THE CHRIST
OF THE
IGNATIAN EXERCISES

JESUS OF NAZARETH YESTERDAY AND TODAY

THE CHRIST
OF THE
IGNATIAN EXERCISES

JUAN LUIS SEGUNDO

*Edited and Translated from the Spanish
by John Drury*

ORBIS BOOKS

Maryknoll, New York 10545

Originally published as *El Cristo de los ejercicios espirituales,* which is Part 3 of Volume II of *El hombre de hoy ante Jesús de Nazaret,* copyright © 1982 by Ediciones Cristiandad, S. L., Huesca, 30–32, Madrid, Spain

English translation © 1987 by Orbis Books
Published in the United States of America by Orbis Books, Maryknoll, NY 10545

Manufactured in the United States of America

English manuscript editor: William H. Schlau

Library of Congress Cataloging-in-Publication Data
Segundo, Juan Luis.
  The Christ of the Ignatian exercises.

  (Jesus of Nazareth yesterday and today; v. 4)
  Translation of: El Cristo de los ejercicios
espirituales.
  Bibliography: p.
  Includes index.
  1. Jesus Christ—History of doctrines—16th century.
2. Ignatius, of Loyola, Saint, 1491-1556.   Exercitia
spiritualia.   3. Spiritual exercises.   I. Title.
II. Series: Segundo, Juan Luis. Hombre de hoy ante
Jesus de Nazaret.   English; v. 4.
BT198.S39213   1987   232'.092'4   87-14186
ISBN 0-88344-570-0
ISBN 0-88344-569-7 (pbk.)

Somewhere in this world there exists a group, a community of persons, with whom I discussed the themes of these volumes one night a week for almost twenty years. We, the members of that group, became more than friends. We became brothers and sisters. By now it is almost impossible for me to say which thoughts are my own and which I owe to others in the group.

Participating in that group were people who became Christians only in adulthood, who were not yet Christians when we were talking about the topics that fill these volumes. But all of us were equally captivated by Jesus of Nazareth, and the quest for him made us even more brotherly and sisterly.

Some members of that community are now far removed in space, though not in affection. Others became part of that reflection and affection at a later date. To all of them I dedicate these volumes, not as a personal gift from me but as a duty honored: a work returned to those who brought it to life.

JUAN LUIS SEGUNDO

Contents

INTRODUCTION

Christologies in Christian Spiritualities

My intention in this volume is to study in close detail one, *only one,* christology: that of the Spiritual Exercises of Ignatius Loyola. Readers may well ask: What is the point of trying to bridge the gap of twenty centuries between us and the New Testament by doing that? What benefit can readers, Christian or not, derive from accompanying me in this exploration?

From the very start of Volume II *(The Historical Jesus of the Synoptics),* I have been stressing one point about the relationship between faith and ideologies. In principle, that relationship makes it impossible for us to establish a science or discipline whose product would be one, single 'christology': i.e., a tract bringing together all our knowledge-data about Jesus. Neither the New Testament nor what we might call the 'absolutization' of Jesus by the Chalcedon formula[1] should turn us away from that well-grounded conviction. The fact is that God, in revealing himself as the *ultimate* sense and meaning of the human being, always does so in a penultimate way: i.e., through a limited existence and project such as those of Jesus of Nazareth. Historically speaking, they cannot be the last. History will continually be posing new challenges to any humanizing tendency. New and unexpected problems will force people to go back and explore more deeply the meaning already discovered, so that it may be both significant and effective in the new context. That is precisely what Paul did with Jesus, as we saw in Volume III *(The Humanist Christology of Paul).*

In the later life of the Christian Church and its *reflection,* we have already noted that it was the divinization of Jesus that gave rise to efforts to establish one christology, one that would be as correct and complete as possible, apparently without any regard for the problems beings faced in real life.

But those problems break through and make their presence felt in all sorts of subtle ways; and the Christian, immersed in history, adapts his or her interpretation of Jesus to the problems actually being encountered even though it may be a costly effort done unwittingly and at the expense of his or her professed theology. To be sure, theology itself is not immune to cultural influences and

1

issues either; but there the connections, logically enough, are more sophisti-
cated and hence less perceptible.

That is why I think it is fitting that we analyze at least one of the christologies
that have been incarnated in the very life of Christians, in their *spirituality*. It
seems to be entirely consistent with what has gone before in these volumes, and
with my overall effort to recapture the significance that Jesus of Nazareth
might have for today's human being.

I

Why do I talk about 'spirituality' here? This word has taken on a technical
sense, due to a sort of division of labor that has occurred. We now find that
christologies are situated on two very different levels, and that we do not
always find clear connection and communication between those two levels:
i.e., the level of theological reflection on the one hand, and that of lived
Christianity on the other.

The latter obviously takes in an enormous range of possibilities: from more
personal christologies that have come down to us through history or literature
because they were lived by prominent personalities, to highly systematized
christologies that have been put into practice in an organized way by numerous
people and over long periods of time. Let me cite just two well-known examples
from Spanish literature to illustrate this difference.

My first example, not quite a century earlier than the work of Ignatius
Loyola, is Jorge Manrique's *Coplas por la muerte de su padre* (c. 1476).[2] It
contains christological elements of enormous interest, not because it offers
specialized study in exegesis or theology, but rather because it offers a highly
personal synthesis; and in that synthesis we can see how the christology lived in
his era was influenced by the centuries-long struggle against the Moors in
Spain. The latter was something unforeseen and even unthinkable for the
authors of the New Testament; but somehow it had to be incorporated into the
christology (i.e., the interpretation of Jesus of Nazareth's significance) fashioned by a man going to war in Jesus' name. And it had to be without any
apparent fissures, as is the case with any successful cultural synthesis.

This is not a unique case, of course. The basis and consistency of the
Crusades were grounded in a specific christology that assumed armed conflict
against the enemies of the faith. I choose Manrique's work as my example here
for two reasons. First, his *Coplas* is a monument of Spanish literature known
to both Christians and Non-Christians. Second, it reflects one of the lay
influences that, along with the monastic influence of Thomas à Kempis, would
have a crucial impact on the soul of Ignatius Loyola and the content of his
Spiritual Exercises.

Manrique's father, a knight who waged war so valiantly against the Moors, is
at the point of death. Sent by God, death knocks at his door and urges him to
submit to God's will. Besides the physical life he has already led and the life of
great fame he hopes for, there is another that is even more important:

El vivir que es perdurable	*Lasting life*
no se gana con estados	is not gained by
mundanales,	worldly estates,
ni con vida deleitable	nor with pleasant living
donde moran los pecados	in which lie the sins
infernales;	of hell;
mas *lost buenos religiosos*	but *the good monks*
gánanlo con oraciones	*gained it by prayers*
y con lloros;	*and tears;*
los caballeros famosos,	*the famous knights*
con trabajos y afficciones	*by labours and hardships*
contra moros.	*against the Moors.*
Y pues vos, claro varón,	And since you, famous warrior,
tanta sangre derramasteis	*spilled so much*
de paganos,	*pagan blood,*
esperad el galardón	you may expect the reward
que en este mundo ganasteis	that you gained in this world
por las manos. . . .	with your hands. . . .[3]

Manrique the Knight, a model of Christian balance as depicted by his son, responds in terms that we might describe as simple and orthodox as those of death:

No gastemos tiempo ya	Let us not waste time now (he answered)
en esta vida mezquina	in this base life
por tal modo,	like this.
que mi voluntad está	For my will is
conforme con la divina	in agreement with the divine
para todo,	in everything;
y consiento en mi morir	and I consent to my death
con voluntad placentera,	with a joyful, clear
clara y pura,	and pure will,
que querer hombre vivir	for it is madness
cuando Dios quier que muera	that a man should wish to live
es locura.	when God wishes him to die.[4]

The orthodoxy of his response comes out clearly in the invocation to Jesus Christ that follows. We seem to be hearing faint echoes of Paul and the hymns to Christ that he, and perhaps John, incorporated into New Testament writings:

Tú, que por nuestra maldad,	*You who, on account of our wickedness,*
tomaste forma servil	*took servile shape*
y bajo nombre;	*and lowly name.*

tú, que a la divinidad	*You who united to Your divinity*
juntaste cosa tan vil	*a thing so vile*
como el hombre;	*as man;*
tú, que tan grandes tormentos	You who have suffered without resistance
sufriste sin resistencia	such great torments
en tu persona,	with Your body:
no por mis merecimientos,	*not for my merits*
mas por tu sola clemencia	*but only out of Your clemency,*
me perdona. [5]	*pardon me.* [5]

It is thus that the knight brings his life to a close, surrounded by his family. And the son ends his *Coplas* on the following note:

que aunque a la vida murió,	Although his life has perished,
dejónos harto consuelo	his memory
su memoria.	has left us much consolation. [6]

This example, I hope, suggests the interest that theology should take in the real, though often hidden, relations between its own theories and whatever amount of them passes into a culture and the life of people immersed in it. But here my example is mainly designed to make two things clear.

The first thing is that christology has pursued its creative course since the New Testament. We may positively or negatively evaluate that course, or any one of its stages, particularly from the standpoint of strict orthodoxy. But the undeniable interaction between culture and faith is surely a sign of life.

The second thing is that these forms of living christological faith, sometimes more personal and sometimes more cultural, do not tend to systematically check out how coherent they may be with theology.[7] But when these forms or ways of living Christianity and seeking perfection in it are structured in a more reflective way within the Church, the result is a more ambiguous phenomenon that often does not get the attention it should.

These various efforts at systematization are called 'spiritualities' in the accepted idiom of theology. Thus we may talk about 'Franciscan' spirituality, 'Carmelite' spirituality, the spirituality of Catholic Action, and even the spirituality of liberation theology.[8]

The ambiguous phenomenon associated with spiritualities is the fact that there often seems to be a secret or hidden tension between two poles. On the one hand spiritualities tend to originate in one of those personal experiences where culture and christology are fused in a living thing, not exactly in opposition to the theoretical or academic teachings of theology but rather without any particular regard for them. In order to ensure that a spirituality will be effective and have a recognized place in the Church, on the other hand, its founder or one of the immediate followers often will attempt to unite both poles. The lived spirituality will be cast in the existing theological molds accepted by specialists, whatever be the level of academic development attained by theology at the time. Or there may be an even more gratuitous reason. The creator of the spirituality may be personally concerned to give it adequate and suitable theological expression, having recourse to the theological categories at hand in order to accomplish that.

The result, in any case, is often ambiguous. The initial personal experience often overflows the banks of a theology, in this case a christology, that was worked up in a laboratory, so to speak. We can detect an unevenness, sometimes a certain lack of coherence, between the two.

The specific object of my study in this volume will provide us with a clear example of all this, but I would simply like to note another brief example here.

What we know as 'Carmelite' spirituality is based mainly on the mystical experiences of John of the Cross and Theresa of Ávila. Now even granting that cultural influences can be subtle and play their part surreptitiously, we can say that Theresa describes her experiences with all the simplicity and freshness with which she actually lived them. In the work of John of the Cross, on the other hand, we detect a deliberate effort to frame his experiences within the accepted theological categories of his day. Thus many of his statements in the first part of the *Ascent of Mount Carmel,* relating to what is commonly known as the 'purgative way', seem to be based on a specific theology of the creature-creator relationship that is, if not alien to the message of Jesus, at the very least superseded by it.

In *The Nature and Destiny of Man* Reinhold Niebuhr looks at two passages from St. John of the Cross that illustrate this curious fact.[9] One, from the *Ascent of Mount Carmel,* views the whole being of creatures as nothing compared to the infinite being of God: "There is nothing in the world to be compared with God, and he who loves any other thing together with Him wrongs Him."[10] The second, from the *Canticles,* reads: "As long as the soul has not attained unto the state of union of which I speak, it is good that it should exercise itself in love, in the active as well as the contemplative life. But once it is established there, it is no longer suitable that it should occupy itself with other works or with exterior exercises which might raise the slightest possible obstacle to its life of love with God, and *I do not even except those works most relevant to God's service"* (Segundo italics).[11]

Niebuhr rightly notes: "Christianity . . . has difficulty in preserving the Biblical conception of love against mystical and rationalistic tendencies to interpret this love in such a way that it becomes purely the love towards God and ceases to be related to brotherhood and community in history."[12]

As I see it, the only flaw in Niebuhr's observation is his lumping of 'mystical and rationalistic tendencies'. He does not seem to realize that the latter alone are wholly and exclusively responsible for the problem. When the Carmelite mystic, John of the Cross, expresses himself freely, he does not separate love for God and love for neighbor the way he does in the above statements. The same goes for other mystics. And we cannot help but be incredibly confused and disconcerted by such statements when we compare them with the concrete, historical, risky, and deeply human life of the man himself.

For all the above reasons, then, I want to study a christology in one of these 'spiritualities'. Less coherent, perhaps, than the 'christologies' lived by historical or literary personages, a christology-become-spirituality tells us more about the course that has been followed in the interpretation of Jesus of Nazareth—in the specialized interpretation of him, if you will.

II

Now I need only introduce my readers a bit more directly to the specific christology we shall examine in this volume. As I explained in the previous section, I think there is value in examining at least one christology embodied in a 'spirituality'. I chose the Spiritual Exercises of Ignatius Loyola because I happen to be more familiar with that particular spirituality. Moreover, it is all the more tempting as an object of christological investigation because it embodies and effectively conveys a christology that seems to have withstood the test of time. Four and a half centuries of theology have washed over the Exercises without any noticeable effect. The little work of Ignatius continues to offer many Catholic Christians the most deeply moving experience of Jesus of Nazareth that they will have in their lives.

But consider this. Vatican II, to mention only one possible example, had much to tell us that was new, unexpected, and practically scandalous to those who knew nothing about possible gaps or holes in earlier theology—not to mention those who did not want to even hear of any such gaps. Given that fact, is it really likely that the Exercises would have come through that shocking ordeal unscathed?

The problem is so obvious that few partisans or directors of the Ignatian Exercises would deny it, as far as I know. But there are two subterfuges, two easy ways out of the difficulty, that are just too tempting for most of them to resist. The temptation is all the stronger insofar as the Exercises, as well as other more superficial and unsound forms of the Christian spiritual life, continue to attract clients amid the uncertainty and loneliness of contemporary urban life.

The first subterfuge, as I see it, is a more or less Illuminist confidence in the life and activity of the Spirit within the Church. This confidence allows people to turn the problem over to theologians. The assumption is that the function of the theologian is precisely that of clearing such obstacles from the road so that the Exercises may keep on producing the same fruits they did in the past. Thus a director of the Exercises may know that Protestant theology and then Catholic theology were confronted with the whole issue of the demythologization of dogma, which is closely bound up with the whole idiom and language of the Exercises concerning God. Ordinarily the director will assume that it is up to the theologian to solve the issue in such a way that the Exercises may proceed on their merry way as usual.

The second subterfuge is more complicated, and I think it needs more explaining for those readers who may not be familiar with the subject. There has been much discussion and debate about the psychological processes that the Exercises set in motion. Indeed some have woven a mysterious network around them when, in fact, they may be only the genial intuition of an *amateur,* who glimpsed a way to bring alive the great themes of Christianity for people in an extraordinarily intense way. One of those themes was, of course, christology.

Whatever one's opinion about that debate may be, it cannot be denied that in their time and place, and according to the criteria then used by the Church, the impact of the Ignatian Exercises was very great. Exceptional personalities were transformed by them into Christians who stood out by virtue of the serious, deep, and total way in which they lived Christianity as it was understood in their day. That is a fact, even if we may find their orientation and outlook debatable today. It is also a fact that the Exercises continue to produce results, due to complicated reasons that are not easy to pinpoint and that are not germane here.

What criteria are we to use in judging those results today, particularly with respect to the interpretation drawn from them insofar as it has to do with Jesus of Nazareth? It is not easy to answer that question unless one first analyzes the theology contained in them. It is hardly likely that the psychological processes can be viewed in isolation from that theology, for example, as if they were a glove that could be passed from one hand to another.

But here is where the second subterfuge comes in. Some hope and expect that the Exercises will be able to follow their beaten path after a few theological modifications have been made in some of the Ignatian formulas scattered here and there throughout the work. Those who direct the Exercises, you see, think that their value lies largely in the fact that they offer two things: general truths of the faith and *a specific method to make them operative and effective.* This is obviously very important in the eyes of the directors, many of whom would feel lost without the detailed and explicit method contained in the Ignatian Exercises. They would not know how to communicate those same truths to people who were not 'exercitants', who were just plain people.

Insofar as the practical valuation of the Ignatian Exercises and their wide-spread use are concerned, one can hardly exaggerate the importance, not of their explicit or implicit theology, but of the fact that this theology and its revitalizing aims were incarnated in an intelligent and detailed method that leaves nothing to chance. With the book of Exercises and the various 'Directions' (that start with Ignatius himself) in hand, even people of minimal creativity can readily feel sure of getting good results and so set out to give them.

Another fact of cultural relevance has had a real influence on the positive valuation and practice of the Ignatian Exercises. Their method has been taught, practiced, and espoused by a religious order largely dedicated to putting them to work; and the members of that order were recruited precisely as a result of their practice. Moreover, that order finds its 'charism' in the

Ignatian Exercises: i.e., the past source and present rationale of its existence. After all, didn't the Exercises provide the criterion that differentiated it from other religious orders and gave it a special place and a singular usefulness within the Church?

But how can one pretend to hold on to the same evaluation today if people debate and dispute the very heart of the Ignatian method of contemplating, acting, and serving: i.e., its explicit interpretation of what Jesus Christ signifies for the human being? What would be left of that charism if, for example, major elements of the christology of the Exercises would have to be considered in opposition to the christological elements imbedded in the ecclesiology of Vatican II?

So we find an interesting thing going on. Some theologians who are quite radical, who find it easy to reject both ancient and modern christologies as inadequate or poorly grounded, prove to be surprisingly uncritical when it comes to the Ignatian Exercises. Either they overlook the problems having to do with the value of the christology that constitutes the crux of the Ignatian Exercises. Or else they are uncritical in confronting and dealing with those problems.[13] A critical approach, which one would regard as perfectly natural, logical, and even somewhat boring in dealing with the christology of an Origen, for example, suddenly is seen as a dangerous hot coal when applied to Ignatius Loyola. It immediately arouses suspicions, misunderstandings, and hostile reactions.

I say all this because some of my readers may focus almost exclusively on the epoch when the christology of the Exercises was elaborated. They may not realize how complicated it is to deal with something that was elaborated in the past but that remains very much alive and relevant today. To many Catholic Christians it will seem more personally or institutionally iconoclastic to challenge and debate the christology of the Ignatian Exercises than to raise questions about the Johannine christology in the New Testament, for example.

One final difficulty is associated with my study of the Ignatian Exercises in this volume: the esoteric nature of Ignatius's Spanish terminology in naming or describing the different stages of the spiritual process in question. Such esoteric terminology is also to be found in other spiritualities, of course. But can readers unfamiliar with this distinctive terminology find any interest or benefit in my treatment of Ignatian christology in this volume, since I cannot take time to explain each and every one of the terms used?

I would say yes, for several reasons. First of all, English-language readers and other foreign readers benefit from the fact that there are careful, accurate, annotated translations in their languages. They need not confront directly the difficult Spanish of Ignatius. When I refer to his titles, moreover, I usually explain their *content* at some point as well. And since references to the specific sections of the Exercises are provided, readers may readily look up the section in question to see what a given phrase refers to.

I would also point out that the book entitled the *Spiritual Exercises,* as far as we know today, was composed in two stages. Most of it was done in the first stage, deriving from the personal experiences of the recently 'converted' knight in the little city of Manresa. The second and smaller part of the book, including perhaps some revisions of the earlier material, dates from the time when Ignatius was studying theology at the Sorbonne in Paris (several years later). Thus we have the seeds of the two elements I associated with any 'spirituality' above: personal life-experience on the one hand, and some bridge or connection between that experience and the academic theology of the day on the other hand. As we have noted already, it is almost impossible that there would be complete consistency between the two elements. Personal experience is normally far richer than the theoretical or intellectual framework one adopts to express it (and oppress it). I shall return to this matter in the Appendix.

I might also note, however, that the volumes in this series are interconnected but relatively independent. If some readers prefer not to read this volume, or to postpone its reading until a later date, they will miss only *one* example of the christologies that have been lived by people between the time of the New Testament and our own day. They should have no trouble reading other volumes as such, and especially following the line of development that runs from my treatment of the historical Jesus (Volume II), to Paul's creative work of christology (Volume III), and then to our present-day task of framing Jesus of Nazareth and his significance in terms of an evolutionary context (Volume V).

•

But my reflection on the christology imbedded in the spirituality of the Ignatian Exercises would not really make any sense unless it were preceded by a brief study of the christological profession of the Council of Chalcedon. For good or ill, Chalcedon is a landmark in the history of christology. Its formulation—'Jesus is truly God and truly human being'—is an achievement that we cannot disown, even though it may have been expressed in the cultural and philosophical categories of a specific age and locale. From the fifth century on, its normative role has remained constant. It was also normative for the different spiritualities that arose, including the Ignatian Exercises. In the latter the meditation on the mysteries of the life of the historical Jesus are governed by a deeply rooted conviction: this Jesus is the Son of God, the Christ. Hence Chalcedon is present in the little work of Ignatius Loyola, and my next chapter on that Council and its issues is very much related to the theme of this volume. It will help us to better understand my treatment of the Ignatian Exercises in the following chapters.

CHAPTER I

Jesus and God: Approach to the Council of Chalcedon

The creation of new and different christologies did not stop when the works making up the New Testament were finished. As we have seen, the New Testament does not present or permit one sole and single interpretation of Jesus' significance. Each of its major works takes up the task of fashioning or refashioning that interpretation in order to get it across effectively to a context with different needs.

However much continuing recourse to the seemingly fixed corpus of Scripture, the New Testament in this case, may have restrained the creative boldness of the Christian community, other inescapable pressures from history kept forcing it to try to recapture anew the significance of Jesus for humanity. These efforts had their logical ups and downs as well as varying degrees of depth and profundity.

For the first four centuries after Christ's death—more specifically, up to the Councils of Nicea (325), Ephesus (431), and Chalcedon (451)—most of this christological creativity focused around giving a complete answer to this question: *Is Jesus of Nazareth God?* Since the answer given was 'yes', emphasis quickly shifted to another question that might seem rather odd to us today: *How?*

Since my focus in this volume and Volume V picks up the issue of christology at a much later date, I should offer my readers a brief review of the earlier historical efforts to answer these questions.[14] Even more importantly, I should try to make clear what those early answers meant for later christologies right down to our own day.

I would remind my readers once again that this five-volume series is not a treatise in *theology*, as the latter term is commonly used today. My aim is to rescue the question of Jesus' significance for human existence from the discipline that has expropriated the task of interpreting Jesus for many centuries, and that has performed it for the exclusive benefit of those belonging to the Christian religion as a whole or to specific Christian Churches.

11

I consider the stress on methodology, characteristic of this series from the very first volume, necessary in order to give back to *any and every* human being the whole question of Jesus' meaningfulness and the possible richness of the answer. At the very least I want to give back the question to those human beings who realize that the way of facing existence demonstrated by Jesus of Nazareth had an impact on history at a certain point in time; and I want to show that this way of his, in translated form, can even today interest and humanize people who, due to cultural misunderstandings or more profound and considered reasons, claim they do not believe in God.

Now it is an historical fact that many formally religious categories have been applied to Jesus from the New Testament on. In Volumes II and III, however, I have tried to make clear that the human significance of Jesus of Nazareth does not depend on accepting the presuppositions of those categories, at least not in the form they have taken in real life today. Thus I have remained faithful to my effort to respond to the challenge offered by Milan Machoveč in *A Marxist Looks at Jesus*. Stripping away esoteric approaches, I have tried to present *a Jesus for atheists* (see Volume II, Chapter II, pp. 13–14). Of course I do not mean a Jesus for atheists alone. I mean a Jesus who can get beyond the traditional barriers of language and categories and thereby reach human beings who are more concerned with what I have called their own *anthropological* faith, who may not think of God at all or who may have rejected the idea of God, the latter perhaps being a distorted idea of God (see GS:19).

In Volumes II and III, I think I have been as sparing as possible in the use of specifically religious terms and arguments. That was possible because in examining the historical Jesus in Volume II and the christology of Paul in Volume III, we found that we needed *keys* to interpret them. A *political* key seemed best suited to the task of Volume II, an *anthropological* key to the task of Volume III; and those keys should be comprehensible to any human being, religious or not.

Even then, in many instances we could not avoid contact with the sacral mentality, language, and categories of Jesus' and Paul's age and culture, which are not ours today. The sacral or religious is not to be equated with the mythical, of course, but what I said about the latter also applies to the former in one respect. We cannot simply reject it as if it had no meaningful content whatsoever for us; instead we must interpret it, trying to understand what is being said to us in that kind of language.

What, then, is the point and purpose of talking here about the question of the divinity of Jesus of Nazareth? Why bother? Is it really necessary *within the framework of my objective in this series*, which differs from that of a 'theology'? Am I not introducing it out of mere habit or routine, thus breaking with the methodological soberness I have been trying to maintain in our quest for the significance of Jesus within the realm of *anthropological* faith, which can or does give direction to the life of any human being?

Here is how I would answer those questions in general terms. My effort in these volumes, which is 'antichristological' in the sense explained in Volume II

(Chapter II), seeks to restore to today's human beings the ability and the desire to *create* christologies, to fashion interpretations of Jesus that give richness and maturity to their lives. To that extent my effort cannot be restricted even to the multiplicity of christologies found in the New Testament.[15] It must keep moving through history, showing how christologies have been succeeding and replacing each other in differing historical contexts despite all efforts to fashion *definitive* systematizations. For reasons indicated above, I can only focus on one christology in this volume. But the basic point holds true in any case, and it is the core of my answer to the questions asked above. From a certain point in time on, roughly the fifth century, we face a new fact. All the new christologies will *expressly* and *methodically* ask the question whether Jesus Christ is God, and will expressly and methodically answer 'yes'.

So if we want to make contact with what Machoveč calls the Christian 'spiritual traditions' of the postbiblical period, and if we really want to have a full understanding of them, we must understand what this question and answer meant to them and what influence they had on subsequent interpretations of Jesus' significance for human existence over the course of many centuries.

Right here at the start I shall indicate that the 'theological' answer to the question about Jesus affected the issue of his anthropological significance in two major ways. Hence I must provide my readers with important data they need to understand what follows.

The christological controversies of the first four centuries resulted in a positive answer to the question about his divinity, though it should be stressed that it was a complex and subtle answer as well. The first way in which this affected later thinking about the anthropological significance of Jesus was to impose something important, which would only show up later as a limitation. Interest in Jesus was reduced or confined to those who fell within a certain spectrum of religious beliefs. Jesus moved to a different level, as it were. To understand and appreciate his significance now, people had to be in basic agreement on such questions as the existence and nature of God. This sort of monopoly is still pretty much accepted without question by contemporary Western culture. That is why Machoveč, for example, had to devote a whole chapter of *A Marxist Looks at Jesus* to explaining why and how a professed atheist could be vitally interested in Jesus of Nazareth.

Here we have the core of the question I should like to consider in this chapter: Was it sound and right that Jesus should be appropriated by religious language, categories, and disciplines?

There is a second way in which the affirmative answer about Jesus' divinity affected later christologies. I shall cover it only theoretically and in principle in this chapter. The rest of this volume will really be an implicit treatment of how it worked out in practice. The question here is: In declaring Jesus to be God, did the Christian community strip him of human traits that are crucial if his significance for human existence in general is to be deeper and more relevant? In this chapter, I shall try to show how Chalcedon tried to avoid that extreme. In the rest of Volume IV, we shall see whether that extreme really was avoided.

I

Some readers may point out that it did not take several centuries after Jesus' death for the question of his divinity to surface on the horizon. It occupied a crucial place in the thinking of his first followers, who recorded the whole problem in their writings from the New Testament on.

Two precautions must be noted here, however. First, this question plays a very different role before and after the paschal happenings, i.e., before and after their experiences with the risen Jesus. Second, the question and answer regarding Jesus' divinity, in the light of his resurrection, respond to very different interests when they are formulated within the perspectives of the New Testament and the immediately following period on the one hand, and when they are formulated to establish a 'digital', dogmatic statement to be considered normative for all later christological thinking. In the dogmatic formulation metaphor is no longer interpreted as metaphor. Insofar as possible, it is stripped of its metaphorical character so that it may take on the precision of an abstract, universal concept.

Let us begin with the question of the historical Jesus, the prepaschal Jesus we studied in Volume II. There we saw that Jesus did not appeal to his personal quality or his special relationship with God to interest his contemporaries and recruit followers. The center of his life and message, the key to his destiny and its logical outcome in death, was the nearness of the approaching kingdom of God.

Several important data from Volume II are relevant here. First, recall the 'messianic secret': i.e., Jesus' refusal to be identified publicly as the Messiah, even though his works might insinuate that anyway. That refusal would not have made any sense if Jesus had wanted to base his preaching on his own relationship to the deity. Second, he clearly refused to interpret his thaumaturgy as anything but a sign of the power associated with the approaching kingdom of God. Third, his followers openly declared that they were drawn to follow him largely by the power that the realization of the kingdom would supposedly confer on them—which does not rule out their basic solidarity with other criteria more essential to Jesus' project. Finally, Jesus engaged in bitter polemics with those who wanted to know precisely what his relationship to God was *first*, so that they might *then* decide whether they should follow him in the transformations that the establishment of the kingdom implied.

All that should logically lead us to a very important conclusion: whatever his witting or unwitting relationship to the divine was, Jesus thought the crucial and decisive thing was the correct sequence of questions that he himself was raising with his message and his activity. *Before* answering the question about his real relationship with God, one had to understand the values implied in his project and opt for them.

It is important that we dwell on this point. Why this priority of one question over the other? Why not intermingle or juxtapose both? As I see it, the answer has to do with the fact that the two questions are on *different logical levels*.

In one of his fascinating dialogues with his daughter that he calls *meta-logues*, Gregory Bateson points up the difference of logical level between a question that can be answered with a metaphor and a question about the signifying quality of the metaphor itself.[16] He takes his example from ballet. One of the ballerinas in *Petroushka* portrays a swan. She is, metaphorically, a swan, a 'sort of' swan, not really but figuratively. But at the same time she is also a human being, a 'sort of' *real* human being characterized by portraying a swan in the ballet.

Now on one logical level, one level of understanding, I can ask: What is that ballerina-puppet? The answer would be that pointed up by the metaphor: a swan. But on *another* logical level I can ask: What is that metaphorical swan, that ballerina in the figure of a swan? The answer in this case is much more complicated, having to do with the function that one human being fulfills vis-à-vis other human beings when he or she is identified with a metaphor, when he or she becomes a living metaphor. In this case, you see, I am asking something like this: What is ballet? Or: What is art?

It would be useless and off base to debate which of the two answers is correct. The difference of logical levels rules out any either/or in this case. Borrowing a phrase from Bertrand Russell, Bateson also calls this a difference of *logical types*. In any case, this difference means that it is impossible for us to answer the second question until we first differentiate it from the first question and answer the latter. Only those who understand the particular, the metaphor executed by the ballerina-swan, can go one step further and understand the universal, i.e., the (metaphorical) function of ballet for human beings.

In a similar way, understanding the particular and concrete project known as the kingdom of God must be differentiated from, and precede, understanding the relationship of Jesus to the deity in general. If we take the logical levels into account, we see that asking whether Jesus is God presupposes we already know what we mean by God. But how can we know that without taking into account the projects that Jesus attributes to God?

Actually this is not an isolated case, not even in the Bible itself, even leaving aside the Old Testament arguments cited by Jesus himself as arguments for the correct sequence of questions. At various points in the Bible we find that two types of questions on different logical levels are superimposed without being confused. Faced with the prospect of imminent exile, for example, Haniah and Jeremiah speak in Yahweh's name but offer two different, opposing views of the future that awaits their nation. Then the prophecy moves to a different *level*. Yahweh addresses himself to Jeremiah once again. This time the prophet-ically inspired content does not refer directly to the future of Israel, however, but to the *criterion* for discriminating between prophecies that depict opposite futures (see Jer 28). In short, the prophetic message now focuses on the consistency of prophecy itself. Prophecy now becomes a prophecy about prophecies. The difference between the earlier prophecy and this one is like the difference between a number and its square, or between a particular member and the genus that contains it.[17]

The historical life of Jesus of Nazareth comes even closer to being a limit-case in this respect. Of the two questions, only one seems to be crucial and decisive: the first one.[18] It is not just that its differentiation from the second question is clearly marked. Insofar as we can distinguish the historical Jesus from the christologies of the Synoptics, we find a certain exclusion of the second question, even though that exclusion may be provisional.

That prompts me to briefly consider a unique case in the Bible which, despite all appearances, is very closely related to that of Jesus in this respect, especially if my interpretation of Jesus' life and message in a *political* key is accepted as correct.

I am referring to a question that theology has been forced to leave without a satisfactory answer because it has gotten caught up in the mistake of confusing or mixing different logical levels: Why does the poem or group of poems known as the Canticle of Canticles (or Song of Songs) figure in the canon of books considered by Israel to be divine revelation?[19]

Let us just look at the Introduction to this biblical book in the *Jerusalem Bible* and see how it poses and answers the issue:

> People have found it surprising that a book that *makes no mention of God* and whose vocabulary is so passionate should figure in the sacred canon. . . . Of all the Old Testament books this has been most variously interpreted. Only two of these interpretations are acceptable. The Jewish rabbis understood it *allegorically*: the relationship of lover and beloved is that between God and Israel, the traditional prophetic marriage meta-phor dating from Hosea. The writers of the early Church, with the exception of Theodore of Mopsuestia, adopted the same explanation, though with them the allegory becomes one of Christ and his Church. This allegorical interpretation is accepted, under various forms, by the majority of Catholic commentators today. . . . Other scholars prefer the more obvious meaning. For them the Song is a collection of hymns to true love sanctified by union. And since God has given his blessing to marriage, the theme is of the *religious* and not merely of the physical order. (JB:991; Segundo italics)

Now the fact is that it is difficult to give rational grounding to either one of these two hypotheses, which cover the spectrum of possible answers. The allegory hypothesis borders on the improbable for various reasons. There is the concrete, luxuriant, and varied nature of the descriptions and situations. There is the fact that we would have a whole book serving as an allegory without anyone's alluding to its character as such within it, which runs counter to the general custom when that literary genre is used in the Bible.[20] There is the marked difference between the amorous content of this book and all the biblical conceptions of the covenant or marriage between Yahweh and Israel, however dissimilar and uneven in their origins or results. An allegory is always a call to attention. It generally entails a certain lack of realism, which calls attention to the fact it is pointing to something other than what it seems to be presenting. But in the Song of Songs, the realism is dense and unbroken.

Even leaving aside the dubious notion that the poem reflects the reality of *marriage* specifically, we note that the second hypothesis is weak for various reasons that more directly relate to our purposes here. It assumes, you see, that God's blessing suffices to turn any supposedly profane or secular theme into a 'religious' one. But God's blessing is not the exclusive patrimony of the marital bond. Genesis tells us that it extends to the whole of creation.[21] Hence any theme would be entitled to be considered divine revelation, whether it speaks of God or not. And in that case the criterion for constituting a divine revelation would have to be extended from a particular thematic content (the religious, God) to some quality or genial ability of the author, pointing up in whatever human area a broader or deeper dimension than we are accustomed to see in it.

But if that is the case, why not prescind completely from the obviously unsatisfactory reason that God has blessed marriage? Why not start from the opposite direction and conclude that the God of Israel can be known only by those who share, with God, the same high valuation of the human that the Song of Songs presents to us?

In Volume I (*Faith and Ideologies*), I undertook a phenomenological analysis to show that faith, as a necessary and omnipresent anthropological dimension, is not divided neatly into two distinct categories: one religious and the other, by virtue of its content, secular or profane. Dovetailing with what we have seen about the Bible, our analysis indicated that the testimony grounding faith is effective to the extent that it is *human*, to the extent that it can point out a suitable road to happiness. Moreover, God cannot stir up faith any other way.

This entails certain consequences that need to be mentioned briefly here. *First:* since we can grant our faith only to a witness who has an impact on us and offers us a way to happiness, any *mixing* of divine or superhuman features in that witness, far from strengthening or reinforcing our faith, will sooner or later eliminate it completely. Insofar as the pathway to happiness presented to us by the witness is conditioned by characteristics, qualities, or powers that a human being cannot possess, the force of the model or testimony is completely wiped out. Human beings will not stake their lives on a pathway that they know in advance to be beyond human capacities and possibilities.

Second: this should shed light on an important aspect of our use of *religious language*. When the latter is not merely *ideological* in the sense explained in Chapter II of Volume I—i.e., a magical technique to realize any set of values— it helps the human being to allude to the *transcendent* character of his or her ontological and epistemological premises, of certain ultimate data and values that organize the rest of his or her life. In that sense there is hardly any basic difference between saying that in one's preferred social system there will be a perfect dovetailing of market needs and the vocational work of every individual, or saying that this dovetailing will be taken care of by an 'invisible hand', or asserting that *God* will not allow those who seek God's kingdom and justice to lack the necessities of life. The *meaning*-content of the latter two statements does not depend on exploring how a hand might act invisibly, or on reaching some agreement about the metaphysical existence of God and God's providence. The latter question belongs to a different logical level that is normally expressed in 'digital' language, whereas the basic meaning-content of the expression depends on 'iconic' language, the kind of language most suited to the transmission of transcendent data and their anthropological function. The use of digital language for such data may be necessary at times; but it entails the inconvenience of presenting what is not verifiable objectively as an objective description that can be tested, thus often producing a confusion of logical levels.

Third: it logically follows from the above that in *myths* containing demigods or divine incarnations we must differentiate two functions of the personage, or better, of the literary genre depicting them. Insofar as the content of some possible anthropological faith is concerned, the *divine* or superhuman aspect of the personage does not count. It is either forgotten or reduced to human dimensions. It is in terms of those human dimensions that the personage is seen as a witness to some road to happiness that one might follow. The divine aspect has a different function. Hence any straight mixing of the divine and human features poses an obstacle to the testimonial value of the personage.

We find a noteworthy example of this in ancient Greek culture and its intricate mythology. It seems to be a fairly well-established historical fact that the *Iliad* and the *Odyssey*, handed down as the basis of Greek education, were for centuries the testimonial source of Greek cultural values.[22] But what portion of these highly mythological works fulfilled that function? Certainly not the adventures of the gods on Mount Olympus as narrated in those works, but rather the adventures of the human heroes. Even in the case of an almost completely invulnerable demigod such as Achilles, the author takes great pains to make readers forget his divine prerogatives and to highlight his 'human' valor and courage. The death of Achilles is foretold, for example; and his valor would be non-existent, or inferior to that of any other warrior, if we focused on his 'divine' aspect, his almost complete invulnerability.

Fourth: what exactly is the function of this divine 'contribution' to such a human figure, since his resemblance to us and our condition is the only thing that can channel and structure a faith capable of giving meaning to our lives?[23] We need not go into profound explorations to find the answer. We soon realize that the religious vocabulary and aspects do not so much form a special category of qualities that are fused with the rest as attribute an *Absolute* dimension to a witness or testimony that is strictly human in itself. To fulfill its function this testimony, no matter how extraordinary it may be or may be imagined, cannot get beyond the barriers of the particular. Those barriers are part and parcel of history as well as of the indispensable character of a life capable of grounding a faith, be it religious or not.

Fifth: we must logically conclude, then, that the appearance of religious language in a representation of faith is of a different logical order or level than the message itself. It is a *metamessage:* a message about the message and how to understand it, about the cognitive and operational level that this faith attains. As I explained in Volume I (Chapter III), religious faith does not consist in transferring our existential wager from a *human* witness to another witness of a *divine* nature, as if both were on the same level and their respective characters could be *mixed*.

So now let us return from these considerations to the case of Jesus of Nazareth. As we know, his preaching constantly operated on a well-defined logical level: the exigencies of the historical project associated with the approaching kingdom of God. The Synoptics tell us that only on one occasion, in the midst of the Galilean crisis, did Jesus cross over from that logical level to a higher one: i.e., when he asked his disciples in private who the people and they themselves thought he was. Their answers already pointed to a privileged relationship between Jesus and God. They thought he was a prophet or *the Prophet*, i.e., the Messiah, the last and definitive agent of God's plans (see Mt 16:13-20). Here again Jesus unexpectedly orders them to keep his identity secret.

In Volume II, Appendix II, we saw that the paschal experiences shifted the historical question about the kingdom to the theological question about the person and divine qualities of Jesus. Here we see clearly and unambiguously the change in logical levels that I have been alluding to; but that does not mean that the change was always effected in a conscious or correct way.

Before we try to evaluate that change, let us look at the process itself and its major implications. To put it briefly, we can say that the message *of* Jesus became a message *about* Jesus. According to Luke in Acts, the initial effect of the paschal experiences after the shock of the cross was to answer a question in the minds of the disciples. That question was not: What *faith* about the kingdom could survive the cross? It was: Had they been *right* to put their trust in Jesus? The shift in logical level here is precisely the same one we saw in the two successive prophecies of Jeremiah (see p. 14).

As witnesses to the resurrection, the disciples report that *the meaning of the Scriptures was opened to them*, and specifically with reference to the Messiahship of Jesus. Even before we examine this simultaneous re-examination of both Scripture and the prepaschal Jesus, we must note that, starting from the resurrection, the discovery of the unique relationship between Jesus and God is verified in all the New Testament documents. It is not explicitated in 'digital' language, however, but rather in 'iconic' expressions of a predominantly poetic nature: e.g., Son of God (with power), Messiah, Lord, Image, Figure, Word, Mediator, High Priest, Alpha and Omega, and God Incarnate.[24]

Bypassing for the moment any analysis of those titles and their meaning, let us focus on one point that takes on its full meaning and importance here. The unconscious shift from one logical level to another is the most common source of the misunderstandings that do harm to the truth and the richness of our thought and action, even when that confusion takes place on a level that is deemed superior (e.g., the religious level). And the fact is that the shift from the message and project of the historical Jesus to the glorification of his person as Messiah and Son of God was not always effected in a well-balanced way. When the levels were mixed and confused, the first question was practically erased by the second.

Here again I invite my readers to compare two passages of Luke. In Luke 4 we find a summary of Jesus' message about the kingdom. In the synagogue of Nazareth he tells the people that the prophecy of Isaiah 61:1-2 has been fulfilled that very day (Lk 4:21). This is the Lukan version of a similar summary, without allusion to Isaiah, in Mark and Matthew: "The time is fulfilled and the kingdom of God is near; change your outlook and believe in the good news" (see Mk 1:15; Mt 4:17).

The second passage comes from Acts, reporting what Peter said to the crowd after the coming of the Holy Spirit on Pentecost. He tells them that Jesus marks the eschatological fulfillment of the messianic hopes as prophesied by Joel. Then he goes on the say:

> "Israelites, hear these words. Jesus of Nazareth, as you know, was a human being whom God accredited among you by the miracles, wonders, and signs that God wrought through him. But you killed him, having him nailed to a cross at the hands of impious people—*him who was handed over in acccordance with God's prior knowledge and deliberate design*. But God resurrected him to life, liberating him from the pains of Hades . . . and we are witnesses to that. . . . Therefore, let the whole house of Israel know that *God has constituted Lord and Christ [Messiah] this Jesus whom you crucified*" (Acts 2:22-24.32.36).

Hearing this statement *about Jesus*, which makes no mention of the arrival or future of the kingdom, Peter's listeners ask what they ought to do. Peter replies: "Have a change of outlook and *let each one of you get baptized in the name of Jesus Christ* for the remission of your sins . . ." (Acts 2:37-38). The account closes with the outcome of this preaching: "Those who accepted his words were baptized. *That day some three thousand were added to their number*" (Acts 2:41).

In other christologies, especially that of Paul (see Volume III), we find a much richer and better balanced integration of the two questions about Jesus. Each seems to contribute elements from its own proper level. Here, on the other hand, we find an unwitting mixture of the two levels. Let us try to get a clearer picture of the *negative* effects of this mixing of levels, since the whole problematic dealing with Jesus still suffers from it today.

Obviously enough, the whole project of Jesus himself is forgotten or overlooked in the discovery of the divine character of his person. The difference between the preaching of Jesus and that of Peter is patent. Peter is no longer summoning his listeners to collaborate in the establishment of God's kingdom. He is asking them to become part of a community whose central content is its agreement about the intimate relationship between Jesus and God: ". . . let each one of you get baptized. . . ."

What Peter says explicitly is even more noteworthy than what he omits. The discovery that "God has constituted Lord and Christ this Jesus" is not linked up with the kingdom or related to it. And retrospectively the struggle of Jesus on behalf of the kingdom is rendered empty insofar as his death is attributed, not to the conflict generated by Jesus for the kingdom, but to 'God's prior knowledge and deliberate design'.[25]

This reply *mixes* two designs of a different logical order in the real life of Jesus: the one that Jesus consciously and deliberately shoulders, and the one that God has for Jesus and other human beings whether they are aware of it or not. Then the very logical conclusion is drawn that the second design is the more valid and significant one in the last analysis, if not the only authentic one. But that does not make any contribution at all to anthropological faith in Jesus Christ, as we have seen. Instead it places his life and message on the plane of ideology as a magical instrument of salvation, or makes them wholly irrelevant for people looking to Jesus for the meaning they might give to their human lives.

This is quite clearly indicated in the outcome of Peter's preaching. Supposedly 'some three thousand' were added to the number of the Christian community 'that day'. This is very curious indeed. The historical Jesus does not seem to have gathered around him much more than one hundred disciples, even giving the latter term the broadest possible connotations (see Acts 1:15). And it is likely that the group around at Pentecost was not much larger than the community of the Twelve, which had been reconstituted after the defection of Judas (see Acts 2:14). Whatever the figure may be, it was certainly small by comparison with the number of new adherents who joined the community at Pentecost.

Investigating the historical Jesus, we notice how hard it was for him to form his disciples. Now, suddenly, Peter's sermon that simply identifies Jesus as the Messiah brings three thousand people to baptism and the Christian community in a single day!

In Volume II we saw the tremendous demands that Jesus made on his disciples. He offered them somber predictions and subjected them to hard tests. There was nothing elitist in that. The plain fact is that the kingdom is very demanding and conflictive; those working to help bring about its arrival must understand and accept the risks entailed in all that. Why does all that disappear suddenly on Pentecost?

Everything suggests that the difference between the preaching of Jesus and that of Peter on Pentecost is not that between a *message* and a *metamessage*. Here it is not a case of the paschal experiences shedding new light on the teachings of Jesus himself. Instead the most conflict-laden elements of the earlier message simply disappear in the mix with the second message. There is no longer any need to know whether people's values fit in with those of the kingdom, however primitively and gradually. The only question now is whether they do or do not recognize Jesus as the Messiah of Israel. The former question could take a matter of months or years to answer, and it could entail concrete manifestations. The latter question is answered in a matter of seconds or minutes.

In Volume III we noted that Paul was much more cautious and profound in confronting the question of Jesus' divine qualities. What that means, I think, is that he is more careful about *keeping the two languages separate*. Intuitively, or perhaps even unwittingly, he somehow senses the difference between message and metamessage. He does not let the latter come across as being on the same level as the former, so that it thereby rides roughshod over the message and wipes out its most central features.

It is true that Paul does somewhat dilute the human and historical density of Jesus by attributing his death, as does Peter on Pentecost, to a divine plan for redeeming humanity from its sins. But this plan does not cause Paul to forget the historical conflict unleashed by Jesus that led to his death, however much he may shift that conflict from a political to an anthropological key. In Paul's presentation, then, the divine design does not annul the importance of the human history of Jesus. Instead it sheds light on it from a different cognitive level.

To anticipate my basic conclusion about the early Councils and Chalcedon, then, I would say the following. The great value of the solutions they offered to the christological controversies of the first few centuries lay in their healthy and tenacious effort, which had to be conscious in some obscure way at least, not to let one of the questions about Jesus get mixed in with the other as if it were on the same level and shared the same *meaning*-content about Christ. In short, they waged a centuries-long battle to maintain the distinction of logical levels with regard to Jesus, and hence the richness and originality of his anthropological testimony.

II

At this point my readers may interpose an objection. Granting all the precautions noted above, they may say that the New Testament itself already affirms the divinity of Jesus. So if we are going to interpret Jesus, must we not enter a sphere reserved to those who possess religious beliefs?

Now the New Testament certainly does affirm Jesus' divinity, though not with the abstract, 'digital' precision of concepts. Its statements remain on a more poetic level, but they do attribute a divine quality to Jesus. Does that mean that faith in Jesus is such only when those approaching him already agree on the fact that God exists and what God is, proceeding from there to see the proper characteristics of a *divine* witness in Jesus? When we approach Jesus, in other words, is our only choice between *religious* faith in him or no faith at all?

We can put this another way. As we saw briefly, the dogmatic formulas of the early Councils do tackle the question of the relationship between the anthropological witness known as Jesus and God. Without necessarily indulging in an improper mixing of logical levels, they say that a divine relationship does exist. So what exactly does the basic question and this positive answer mean?

Speaking in general terms, which will be clarified and specified by the following considerations, we can say that the overall opinion of the New Testament is that 'Jesus is God'.[26] The *literary genre* of this affirmation in the New Testament, however, is very different from that of the dogmatic definitions that find their culmination at Chalcedon.

Let me give two examples, one more abstract and the other more concrete, to illustrate the basic difference involved.

The formula A = B is an example of information, but it does not tell us whether the *source* of the information lies in knowledge of the subject A or knowledge of the predicate B. Everything, in other words, depends on my knowing either A or B first. If I know A, then I will know B; and vice versa.

This brings us to a crucial finding in our case. It is not the *sequence* in which I put the words in the phrase, 'Jesus is God', that tells me which is the known term, the one shedding light on the other. But that is not yet the whole story.

Suppose the predicate does not pertain to the order of description. Suppose it has to do with the realm of anthropological faith, with the values a person now holds after choosing among the various possible paths to happiness. Suppose the statement now reads: 'A is important'. If I do not know A to begin with, the predicate will not help me one bit to describe the content of A, its objective characteristics. Why? Because the predicate refers to a *third* factor not present in the statement: a subject who is *offering an evaluation* of A.

But even though the statement leaves me in ignorance about the reality of A, it is not devoid of sense or meaning. It tells me the place that A occupies in the values-system of the speaker, whom we may call X. And this applies, of course, whether the predicate is 'important', 'very important', or even '*absolutely* important'.

To fully understand the statement, then, I must first know (by other means) object A, so as to be able to understand (thanks to the statement) why 'important' is predicated of A, and thus (again thanks to the statement) come to know the values of speaker X, who thinks A is important.

Lest all this seem like abstract and irrelevant gibberish, let me offer a more concrete example from the Bible. Actually it predates and anticipates Jesus' argument with the Pharisees about the proper premises for approaching the task of interpreting divine revelation and the Law. Those premises, as we have seen, can only be human values already held. Commenting on a passage in Jeremiah, José Míguez Bonino cites a passage from a work by G. J. Botterweck:

> In the writings of the pre-exilic prophets as well as in certain sections of the Wisdom literature, the *knowledge of God* means a religious-moral form of conduct of men towards Yahweh: *to know God* means to 'renounce' sin and the worship of idols, to 'return' to Yahweh and to 'seek' for him, to 'depend' upon him and to 'fear' him; it means to 'practice love, justice and righteousness'. He who *knows God* walks in his ways. *Knowledge of God* is active piety.[27]

Míguez Bonino offers this apt comment on the passage: "This is well said. But it is not enough. It still reflects the 'both-and' formula which we love to use when we don't know how to integrate things which in the Bible are one."[28] The Bible, you see, views knowing God and acting in a certain way as one thing. This shows up clearly in a well-known passage of Jeremiah where the prophet is addressing King Jehoiakim in the name of Yahweh. Comparing Jehoiakim's conduct to that of his father, King Josiah, Yahweh says of the latter: "He judged the cause of the poor and the needy" (Jer 22:16). Míguez Bonino goes on to say:

> And, in a striking sentence, the prophet asks: "Is not this [i.e., Josiah's way of behaving as king] to know me?" Surprised exegetes usually comment that these actions are 'the consequence of', or 'a sign of' knowing God. The text simply confronts us with the bold question: 'Is not this to know me?'[29]

This biblical tradition perdures to the end of the New Testament (see 1 Jn 2:3.49; 3:1.6; 4:6–8.16). If we take it seriously, we must conclude that in the statement, 'Jesus is God', the known term shedding light on the other is *Jesus*, his history, and his activity. Only by doing something similar can we actually experience what would constitute information carrying over to the other term, *God*.

It is important for us to realize that when we hear the above statement or one similar to it, we spontaneously locate the source of information in what appears to be the predicate (*God*) and see the obscurity in *Jesus*. It is Jesus' relationship to God that seems to be obscure. In other words, we think we already know who or what God is, and we understand the statement as a response to the question whether Jesus does or does not possess the characteristics included in the concept, 'God', which is at bottom a generic concept.

As we shall see in the next section, that is how language will function in the christological controversies prior to Chalcedon. But that is *not* how it functions in the New Testament and, I would add, in its immediate environs.[30]

The valid consequence of what we have seen so far is this: if the concept, 'God', must be empty in a certain way, and if it is the attitudes of Jesus that are to give it content, then *no acceptance or rejection* of a specific and 'full' (so to speak) concept of God can be adduced as conditioning acceptance or rejection of the statement 'Jesus is God'. Only after the concrete, historical characteristics of Jesus are introduced into the concept of God can we logically arrive at a 'yes' or 'no'.

Some readers, however, may quite rightly point out that if the concept, 'God', does not have some minimum content of its own, then it will not have any as information either. Hence the 'yes' or 'no' response to it will be meaningless because the statement is a mere tautology: 'Jesus is Jesus'. And we know that a tautology of identity does not constitute any information.

That is why, in the abstract examples offered at the start of this section, I

spoke about a statement in which the predicate serves to transmit an evaluation, to give information about a value: 'A is important'. As we saw, in such a
statement there is a twofold communication: the subject denotes (in code) what
is valued, and the predicate connotes (again in code) the value that is attributed
to the subject. This is the first part of the communication. But since the value,
the ought-to-be, is not in the objects, is not part of their objective description, I
said that the statement necessarily implies another subject different from both
the grammatical subject and the predicate: i.e., the person *for whom* A is
important.

Now let us get back to what we have just seen about biblical language. If
what we have just seen about the typical biblical language on these matters is
correct, if it identifies behaving in accordance with a certain hierarchy of values
and knowing God, then we must conclude that in *this type of language* the
concept 'God', rather than being something that *anyone* could know in its
essence and that, *in addition*, would possess and impose certain value-
judgments,[31] is, in the first place at least, the predicate connoting the *absolute*
character of a specific value associated with an equally specific line of conduct.

Let us test this with the Johannine statement that appears as a consequence
of the preceding statement that Jesus is God: i.e., the statement that "God is
love" (1 Jn 4:8.16). The interpretation of this strange definition has a long
history, but the essential matter can be stated briefly. If the concept of God is
taken to be known in advance, and as something whose content includes
certain objective characteristics such as infinite perfection, immutability, self-
sufficiency, simplicity, and happiness, and if on the other hand it is equally
assumed we know what love (*agapē*) is in the experience of a human life, then
we can only conclude that the Johannine statement is misleading, if not
downright mistaken.

The fact is that the two concepts cannot coincide. The well-worn tack of
exegesis, then, would be to pare down the content suggested by human experience for the word 'love' until it *seemed*[32] to be compatible with the predeter-
mined characteristics of God's essence.

But the contradiction would always remain in that type of language. Applicable to human predicates about God is the statement that Lateran IV made
(without weighing its linguistic consequences): "Between Creator and creature
one cannot talk about similarity without at the same time talking about an even
greater dissimilarity" (DS:432). Quite aside from that fact, the author of the
Johannine letter we are considering here discredits any such interpretation; and
he does so in a thorough and radical way. Opposing the cognitive universality
that ought to have been granted to the concept 'God'— open to both the good
and the wicked and independent of any individual's conduct—he states that the
search for the meaning of the phrase must begin from precisely the opposite
direction: "*One who does not love does not know God*, for God is love" (1 Jn
4:8).

In other words: one who does not have the (earthly) experience of love
(*agapē*) cannot form the correct concept of God and employ it in a statement

such as 'God is love' or 'Jesus is God'. The semantic route is the reverse: from actual experience will come the content that is to be given to the term 'God'.

If, then, the statement that Jesus is God is equivalent to saying that Jesus, with the values iconically represented in his life, constitutes the Absolute for me, then the language gains something in clarity and meaning. Let us pause for a minute to examine these advantages, which are basically two.

First, this kind of language makes clear that the faith invested in Jesus interprets the content of his life as an absolute. All the statements that equate or identify Jesus with God bear witness to the fact that the faith invested in him refuses to *seek beyond him*. Please understand this correctly: it does not mean that it seeks nothing *after* encountering Jesus. The human testimony of Jesus is limited. The values transmitted through him are incarnated in an 'ideology' that will oblige people at every moment to rethink and re-create it with the appearance of every new context. But, and this is what I mean to get across here, there is an existential wager placed definitively and totally, so long as this faith lasts, on the significance of Jesus for human existence. Every crisis, failure, or doubt will not be a reason to look for other witnesses. Instead it will be an occasion for going back and interrogating the witness that is identified with the one in whom one has invested an absolute confidence.

The second advantage of this language, quite aside from its fidelity to the data presented to us in the New Testament, is that it confronts *every human being*, religious or atheist, with the question of Jesus. Why? Because the *absolute* character that can be taken on by anthropological faith in a witness does not depend on prior acceptance of the existence of an infinite being with specific (metaphysical) characteristics.

These two advantages notwithstanding, there is something lacking in a language that identifies God with the absolute character that is given to the adhesion typical of an anthropological faith. Saying that Jesus is of absolute importance for me does not coincide exactly with the language used in the New Testament to claim that he is God even though, as we have just seen, it may be the door that opens the way for us to arrive at a basic interpretation of that language.

But before we move on to an analysis of this 'something more', we do well to stress the importance of the conclusion we have just reached. Strange as it may seem, from the Old Testament to the New Testament there runs a line that prevents us from regarding the 'religious' language used there as dependent on a prior knowledge or acknowledgment of God. On the contrary, a specific type of human life or conduct is called 'knowing God', whereas other types, however 'religious' they may be, are radically disqualified in their possible claim to maintain a correct knowledge of God even while entailing mistaken behavior.[33]

III

But there is something more, as I said. It is not just that the Bible tells us that there are as many 'gods' as there are values-systems that a human being can set up to structure its active existence. And that only one of those wagers coincides with the one which ultimately—eschatologically, we would say—will be revealed to be the valid and correct one, the one that had to be maintained *absolutely* in spite of all the failures, doubts, and apparent successes offered by existence.

If that were the case, if everything came down to adopting more or less blindly a specific anthropological faith, the one which would end up being rewarded in the lottery of reality, then the human being would have no clue or criterion for choosing it reasonably. It would be sheer believing for the sake of believing, an unreasonable risk, what has been technically labelled 'fideism'.

It is here that what I have called 'transcendent data' enter the picture and play their crucial role. As I noted, experience cannot give human beings certain elements regarding the ultimate possibilities of reality, and yet they need those elements to structure their world of values in a reasonable way.

Let us pick up from the previous section the conclusion that Jesus, in his 'ideologically' limited life and message, revealed that the absolute for him was love. But how did reality deal with him? According to history, which Paul universalized by converting it into an anthropological dimension, the love of Jesus shattered against certain limits of the real world. And those limits were all the more powerful and even victorious insofar as Jesus' love was more generous, gratuitous, and profound, taking sides with the poor and marginalized against established society and its protected favorites.

How is it possible, then, to put an absolute faith in this *failed* witness, in one whom we could almost say was 'essentially' a failure? Reason will not be the decisive thing here because we are no longer in the realm of science and the universally valid, but reason does exact its rights and demand logic of us. It must be an inner logic, the only kind that is capable of validly and effectively structuring our existence around the set of values presented by Jesus.

As I noted, on this plane, too, reason handles or works with *data*, except that these data are different from the data that make up the realm of science, i.e., from empirical data. And I might add that of these *data* related to Jesus on the one hand and the limits of reality on the other, some are prepaschal, such as the proximate coming of the kingdom that is destined to bring happiness to the poor and marginalized of Israel, and others are postpaschal (or better, paschal), such as the experiences that the disciples had of the new, glorious life of Jesus a few days after his death (see Volume II, Appendix I, pp. 166–77).

Now as I have indicated, transcendent data do not arise from mere observation or from the fact that one sets certain values above others. Hence neither simple contemplation of the sequence of events marking the life of Jesus (including among them the 'apparitions' of the risen one) nor mere attraction to the value that dominates his life (love unto death) is enough to lead us to a reasonable conclusion that we are faced with the transcendent datum by very name: i.e., that Jesus is God or, if you prefer, that the ultimate reality was manifested to us in him.

Jesus appears historically as a human martyr for a human cause. If his disciples 'comprehend' that he is more than that, this is due to the fact that they are connected with a tradition made up of a historical process of deutero-learning; in that process interminable crises and searching gradually discover and connect transcendent data relating to human existence in the most logical and coherent manner possible.

Thus the resurrection of Jesus itself could have been rejected as an illusion, or merely understood as a magical effect, if it had not been preceded by a tradition based on the idea of a growing commitment—covenant—between the Absolute and humanity. And this to the point where the exigency that Peter recalls after Easter, to underline the character of Jesus as 'absolute hostage', will be intimately linked with this series of data: "You will not permit your *holy one*[34] to experience corruption" (Acts 2:27; see Ps 16:10).

At the same time, however, this empirically unverifiable certainty, this transcendent datum, arises from the crisis of another more superficial conception of the convenant between humanity and God. In the latter conception it was assumed that God had to recompense human beings for their good or evil deeds within the limits of their physical lifetime. When repeated and deepened experience (e.g., Job) of the suffering of the just obliged some to seek further, there arose the datum of a justice that somehow must confront death and win out over it. Without this whole journey, simultaneously painful and enriching, without this whole process of penetration into the relations of the Absolute with experience, Jesus would not have been related to the divinity, as he was, or identified with it.

Now once this essential piece was fitted into place, many other pieces belonging to the historical life of Jesus[35] are situated on a similar level. One example is his claim to surpass the Law and to dictate the presuppositions for its correct interpretation.

To sum up: the New Testament writers are convinced that divine attributes suit or apply to Jesus in some way that they do not explain in metaphysical terms.[36]

Before proceeding further, let me put things in balance. This sort of faith in Jesus is what I have called '*religious* faith'. But the qualification 'religious' was not meant to put it beyond the reach of those who, for whatever reason, declare themselves to be areligious or atheists. I would attribute the characteristic 'religious' to an anthropological faith that reaches the point where it enters into a process of learning to learn with respect to transcendent data and ends up putting absolute trust in the witnesses of that same process (see Volume I, Chapter III, section II).

To say it again, I do not consider this faith to be 'religious' because it *talks about God*, i.e., because it employs a universal and metaphysical concept of a transcendent being. It is not religious by virtue of its content. It is religious because it attains a degree or quality of irreversibility in its adhesion that, in terms of language, creates a God, an Absolute, and definitively entrusts the whole existence to that absolute.

Hence I maintain—and the example of Machoveč is illustrative—that an atheist can have this type of faith, contrary to a commonplace notion that has become deeply rooted in our culture. Unless the atheism of the person is not just mere agnosticism or a practical attitude but the consequence of metaphysical reasons that *are opposed* to any of the transcendent data provided by those spiritual traditions: in our case here, to those implied in the testimony of Jesus as interpreted from the standpoint of the whole biblical process. Examples of such opposition would be Camus's vision of the universe as absurd (i.e., meaningless) and any type of mechanistic or deterministic materialism (official Marxism) that says human freedom is illusory.

Having made clear this point, which is to be added to the points brought out in the previous sections, we cannot deny that at least some of the New Testament writers were aware that the divinity of Jesus, especially in the Greek context, posed the problem of properly reconciling his *concrete history* with the most widespread and purified metaphysical concept of God.[37] Thus began a problem that for centuries, up to Chalcedon, would be the object of divisions, polemics, and philosophical and linguistic searching in the Christian communities. We cannot bypass or overlook the issue.

IV

In contemporary theology we find what is practically a 'dogma' about the Council of Chalcedon, which ended for centuries the principal christological controversies among Christians. Surprisingly, however, this 'dogma' is not the one established by Chalcedon. Rather, it is that the formula of Chalcedon is surpassed.

Speaking very generally, we can say that there would be nothing extraordinary about that if it did not seem that the main attacks of present-day theology on ancient dogmatic expressions were concentrated precisely on the Chalcedon formula. To continue in force, after all, formulas necessarily incorporating the cultural and linguistic elements of one epoch must resign themselves to changes matching those introduced by time into the very same cultural and linguistic categories. Furthermore, it is a universally recognized principle in theology that the truth of an ancient formula does not canonize, or thereby preserve as true, the philosophy or ideology that made it possible.[38]

All that must be valid for the formula coined at Chalcedon. Speaking in broad terms, since the Greek terms do not correspond precisely to ours, we can say that the Chalcedon formula established that Jesus possessed two natures, one divine and the other human, in one single person. The two natures, complete and finished in themselves, made him a fully human being without at the same time ceasing to be perfectly or completely God. But the personal unity or oneness meant that Jesus, despite his two natures, was one single person: i.e., the Son of God, he himself God as are the Father and the Spirit. The Chalcedon formula added something important: that the two natures, the divine and the human, were not separable (as if he were two beings united only accidentally), and in like manner neither were they intermingled in the personal oneness to fashion a sort of demigod.[39]

This formula, as I said, bears the marks of its age. This is especially so, as we shall have occasion to see, in its inherent presuppositions about knowledge of the divine nature, where it is especially dependent on the philosophy of the time. But as I see it, the attacks to which it has been subjected are excessive. For it vigorously and courageously maintains the balance that is strictly necessary if we are to think of Jesus as God without thereby obliterating the features, meaning, and relevance of his history as human being, of his being a *witness for us*. Thus it has the no small merit of keeping open the road for further and incessant searching into the anthropological meaning of Jesus' life and message, insofar as it did not subordinate the latter to the prior acceptance and understanding of a metaphysics relating to the divine.

I would first like to reflect on this crucial contribution of Chalcedon, and then show how the presuppositions of its age put difficulties, in practice, in the road it had left open in principle.

(1). We must realize that declaring Jesus of Nazareth to be God was not an easy enterprise in terms of *language*. Considering that language is created by human beings and can never rise above this origin, which gives it meaningfulness, we may ask: What was it trying to say with this formula, assuming that it was trying to say something meaningful? In that apparently simple and clear expression, how would it be possible to avoid the contradiction or the coarse use of 'anthropomorphisms' that inevitably, after passing through the filter of reflection, would lead to the disappearance of the native and imported Greco-Roman gods of Olympus?[40]

First, if we consider the matter closely, we see that the Chalcedon formula implies that since there was no mixture of natures, nothing could be seen in Jesus that was not *human*. We are not to confuse or equate 'perfectly or completely human being' (*perfectus homo*) with a 'perfect human being' (*homo perfectus*), i.e., with someone who escapes the limited human condition and thus permits people to verify empirically his divine condition.

How or what this 'divine nature' of Jesus is exactly is not described in the Chalcedon formula. *In principle*, it leaves open two doors of cognitive access: either we arrive at it by way of philosophy (metaphysics); or we arrive at it through the actual history of Jesus, human as it is but of course connected with the whole biblical process.

Second, the distinction, without mixture, of the two natures certainly offered some defense already against the undue invasion of metaphysical thinking into the human history of Jesus. But the oneness of his person, of his *divine* person, did even more: it involved a further step in the same direction. The fact is that here Chalcedon touched upon the problem of *language*, and did so explicitly.

I am alluding here to the very basis of something called the *linguistic communication (communicatio idiomatum)* between God and humanity in general, thanks to the case of Jesus, which had already been established at the Council of Ephesus (DS:116). Jesus, perfectly or completely human being in terms of his human nature, had been born and had grown up, struggled, suffered, and died. But the linguistic *subject* of all those verbs, strictly speaking, had to be his person. And his person was that of the Son of God, God himself. Therefore, in Jesus and through Jesus, one had to say, and rightly, that God himself had been born and had grown up, struggled, suffered, and died.

It is certainly true, as we shall see, that in the history of Christianity this linguistic route would often be traversed in the opposite or wrong direction; and that only the most obvious exaggerations of that tendency—e.g., transferring to Jesus the supposed impassibility or pure spirituality of the divine— would be perceived and condemned.

But that was not the direction that permitted the *communicatio idiomatum*, i.e., the oneness of language grounded on the oneness of Jesus' divine person.[41] As the Chalcedon formula tells us, this linguistic communication does not operate by *mixing* the natures. The only thing that is rendered possible linguistically is attributing to—or, in grammatical terms, predicating of—the divine *person* what showed up in the humanity of Jesus. In other words, we are talking about a linguistic road that travels in only one direction.

With this, and even though it has not always understood the matter correctly and applied it properly, the Christian community maintained its fidelity to the biblical teaching regarding the 'practical' character of knowing God.[42] Only existential valuation agreeing in its main lines with that of Jesus of Nazareth could permit people to know how or what exactly God was in reality.

Third, it is proper to point out here, if only in passing, another consequence of the linguistic balance of the Chalcedon formula. It is this: *all theological* language, without being impoverished thereby or diminished in the slightest, has to be, at the same time and for the very same reason, *anthropological*—not because of the unconscionable audacity of human beings but because of the incommensurable audacity of God.[43] Because God, in God's very existing, makes possible and endorses that kind of language.

Hence the importance (which we have already noted in Volumes II and III) that both Jesus in the Synoptics and Paul in his major letters give to the basic attitude called *faith* by Paul: i.e., that human audacity which, only by betting on certain human values above everything else, can know God and possess the epistemological premise needed to recognize and accept revelation. With more literal orthodoxy but less audacity, people pass right by Jesus, today as yesterday, without recognizing in him anything that relates him in a very special way to the Absolute.

(2). So where exactly may we find the alleged flaw or obsoleteness of the Chalcedon formula?

As we shall see right now, I think that the negative consequences following Chalcedon and the difficulties we experience with it even today do not really stem from the Chalcedon formula itself but from overlooking or neglecting some of its elements.

As I have already noted, it is often assumed that these problems lie in the 'barbarity' of its expression, which attempts to make the incompatible compatible and does so with linguistic instruments that are too primitive, if not downright ambiguous.

Everything seems relatively clear in it until we ask about something that is more subtle, less *thing-oriented:* i.e., the real consciousness or awareness of Jesus. In the mentality of the age, two perfect natures presupposed two different centers or sources of operation: two subsistences or *hypostases.* Each had its own knowledge and will. For modern human beings, however, person-ality has shifted toward the pole of the *awareness or consciousness* of self that a human being has (and that is assumed for God as well), toward the conscious *ego* that permits the human being to situate itself as the subject of its own acts in the succession of time.

Now consciousness forms part of knowledge, the object of which embraces more than self-knowledge. Hence it would follow that Jesus had two different consciousnesses (two self-knowledges), two distinct *egos*. In that case, what could there be to the personal unity we are being told about? Moreover, if two (metaphysically as well as grammatically) distinct *subjects* are admitted, that logically brings crashing down the linguistic communication that is a crucial consequence of the Chalcedon formula.

Obviously, one could argue that all human investigations attempting to imagine what might have taken place inside that unique being Jesus, *perfectus Deus* and *perfectus homo*, would be pointless complications because of their object and his mystery; that it would be preferable to attend purely and simply to the negative specifications of the Chalcedon formula instead.

But we have a long and very promising road to travel before we can appeal to mystery with full justification. In particular, we must make two points or specifications that are closely linked. Although they may point up certain limitations of the philosophical presuppositions of the Chalcedon formula on the one hand, they will also make clear its basically sound judgment on the other.

First: I noted above that the Chalcedon formula seems to have left two roads open, in principle at least, to knowing what the 'divine nature' possessed by the Son of God might be, the 'divine nature' possessed by the *person* who assumes, in Manrique's phrase, the 'servile shape'[44] of Jesus of Nazareth. The two roads or approaches would be the philosophical or metaphysical on the one hand, conceiving a nature corresponding to the infinite being, or the historical on the other hand, whereby Jesus himself, with his life and message, would show what this nature actually was.

At first glance, however, the second approach seems to be ruled out by the Chalcedon assertion that the two natures are not mixed. That would lead us to the conclusion that the human realities seen in Jesus tell us nothing about his divine nature.

But the actual situation is really this. Before Chalcedon, and even after as we shall see in this volume, the concept of 'nature', understood as that which perdures unalterably amid the changes taking place in finite, observable be-ings, was applied without further ado to God. It was assumed that God had to have a nature of God's own just as a rock, a thing, a tree, and a human being have their own natures.

It is no secret that Greek philosophy, from which this notion came, was always essentialist and even 'thingist', perhaps because it began its journey through what we today would call the first attempts of the *natural* sciences. That is why it almost completely lacks viewpoints about the person and freedom, for example, that later philosophies have brought out.

A point that we must keep very much in mind with regard to our problem is that the identity between the essence and the nature of a being is not total at the level of finite beings; at least it is not at the level of human beings. Hence freedom, which is not supplementary but *essential* to the human being, means that the human being at least partially *gives itself* its own nature. But of course it has limits that can be overcome only with great difficulty or not at all.

It is important to note that as we ascend the chain of perfection of beings, we know less and less about their existence by merely classifying their nature. The ancients defined *homo* as a 'rational animal'. That certainly allows us to draw some valid conclusions about the limits that human activity will never be able to exceed, at least not without going out of its 'natural' classification.

Thus, if we can say that certain kinds of mammals will never be able to fly, the reason is that they, being inferior in ontic perfection, will never be able consciously and freely to alter their body or their environment enough to adapt to flight. But we cannot draw the same conclusion about the human being. And the resultant vagueness surrounding human 'nature', as an indication of what a human being can or cannot do, is precisely the effect of humanity's perfection, not of its contingency or finitude.

Now in the Chalcedon formula there is, to some extent, a mixing of the metaphysical elaborations of the two great Greek currents, the Platonic and the Aristotelian, especially the former. They agree in imagining God more as an infinitely perfect 'thing' than as a completely free being, incomparably freer than *homo* to choose what he *wants to be*. Thus imagined, the 'divine nature' becomes a network of negative characteristics, of things *incompatible* with one's notion of God, such as undergoing movement (the 'unmoved mover'), change, suffering, and relating.[45]

The very notion of the 'creation' of the universe, especially of a material universe, seemed to contradict the divine nature. One had to have recourse to a demon or demigod, a 'demiurge', to imagine it, not noticing that the contradiction would persist even with a minimum of investigation into the ontic origin of such a creator-creature.

Chalcedon apparently overcame this difficulty with the notion of 'linguistic communication'. Thanks to the 'human nature' of the person of the Son of God, one could say of him that he had been born, had suffered and died. But it concealed the problem of the Incarnation lying right there. Was this a real *change* in God, or was it merely an illusory anthropomorphism? If it was a real change in God, that would seem to be incompatible with the divine nature. If it was an illusory anthropomorphism, that would be incompatible with the linguistic communication it purported to establish.[46]

The purity and radicalness of Chalcedon's logic would have been safe-guarded better if there had been available philosophical instruments that permitted it to give freedom its full ontological sense and import. And by freedom I mean the growing flexibility that should be introduced into the concept of nature, the possibility of giving oneself the nature one desires as one ascends the scale of beings. In this way, the plenitude of this characteristic could be located in the divine.

Second: it must be noted that the divine nature (as well as the human nature) personally possessed by Jesus, the Son of God, is something that does not surface from any metaphysical consideration but from *history*, as we see in the Bible.

In the ages when Greek philosophy prevailed, and right up to our own age, people sought to give a metaphysical interpretation to Yahweh's response to Moses in the Book of Exodus when Moses asked for his name. Using a play on sounds more than on words, the Elohist writer has Yahweh replying: "I am who I am" (Ex 3:14). Supposedly, Yahweh was thus informing Moses that his essence is to exist necessarily, without limit or measure.

More thoroughgoing and recent studies have led the majority of exegetes to a different interpretation, one that is much more in line with Hebrew thinking. It also seems more credible, even in translation. To cite one example that will suffice for many, here is part of the relevant commentary on the verse in the *Jerusalem Bible*:

> In semitic thought, knowledge of a name gave power over the thing named; to know a god's name was to be able to call on him and be certain of a hearing. The true God does not make himself man's slave in this way by revealing a name expressive of his essence; this refusal to reveal is contained in the formula *Ehyeh asher ehyeh* ('I am who I am', 'I am what I am') which, in the third person, becomes Yahweh, 'He is'. Understood in this fashion, the name does not define God; nevertheless, for Israel it will always call to mind God's great deliverance of his chosen people and the divine generosity, fidelity and power that prompted it. (JB:81)

In other words, the response is first an evasive or negative answer, as the context brings out, meaning: 'I won't tell you'. But it also suggests that to gain knowledge of Yahweh one must look and see what Yahweh is *for* this people in history. In biblical revelation, then, Yahweh will always show up, not as the Being, but as a human being—only one who is better, wiser, and richer in his projects and relations than human beings are. Which is to say, Yahweh shows up as a project going before the human being and showing it the way to its humanization.

And I say 'as a human being' because Yahweh actually appears to share life with human beings, living through their adventures with them. Yahweh is historically involved and committed, as the 'divine nature' conceived by the Greeks could not be. History, at least the history of Israel in the Old Testament, is *Yahweh's* history. And in it Yahweh feels joy, gets sad or angry, intercedes, and binds himself to human beings by covenants.

If some readers claim that this is nothing more than poetic language, they are certainly right. But beware and take careful note! The language of metaphysics presenting God as the 'unmoved mover' is nothing more than bad poetry from start to finish. It is false poetry: false for presenting as descriptive language what is not that, and also false for not observing the elementary laws of logical language.

Precisely here we find a defect—perhaps the only one—in the Chalcedon formula. The flaw or defect may have been inevitable in its context; forgetting or overlooking the fact that, however necessary digital and logical language may be for the realm of meaning, there are elements in that realm that are made possible only by an iconic language—and not just any kind of iconic language. The language of the two natures is certainly correct. But it is incapable of expressing certain kinds of human experiences, the only ones that can usher us into the 'divine' significance of Jesus of Nazareth.

As an example, let us consider the kind of adventure involved in living a *double 'cultural* nature' as we find it in the phenomena of acculturation. Obviously, there are major differences by comparison with the case of Jesus and his two natures: not only because a culture constitutes a 'nature' only in a certain way and to a certain extent, but also because even the most fluid and universally sensitive of cultures will always be limited, fixed, and static to a considerable degree. That is precisely why it will be recognized as a culture.

Even granting that, we know that authentic, effective acculturation takes place not by mixture (which always proves to be counterproductive), but by an apparent suppression or discontinuance of the first culture in order to acquire the second. But, in turn, the second culture is assumed, grasped, and understood by a person who has lived the first culture, obliging the latter to develop and move outside its routine limits.

Here we have one of those shifts from map to territory, one of those violations of the 'due' separation of logical levels, that necessarily causes a difficulty—evidently present in Chalcedon—in using the digital language proper to logic consistently right to the end.

Now the New Testament itself, especially on two occasions where a high degree of creativity is evident, informs us that the *revelation* which took place in Christ entailed, *for God,* assuming human nature and the adventure of living as a human being—really and truly, without cheating. Except that the 'divine nature', which persists in Jesus without mixture, is totally at the disposal of the divine freedom engaged in the adventure. It is not a limit, as was the first culture in our previous example. It is not something *other*, in the sense of having elements alien to the existence assumed. *It does not lie in what is not human in Jesus but precisely in his way of being human.*[47]

One occasion, not the first chronologically, where the New Testament broaches the crucial issue is the Prologue of the fourth Gospel. After establishing that the Word of God is God, i.e., possesses a divine nature, the Prologue depicts the word under the metaphor of the Light that 'was coming into the world' (Jn 1:9)—according to the most likely version or punctuation—until the Word finally divests itself of its divine attributes and becomes human (Jn 1:14).

It may seem strange to say that the Word divests itself of its divine attributes, but that shows up clearly in the other major text we shall consider. It is Paul's passage in Philippians, where he writes about *kenosis* ('emptying'). But even in the Johannine text itself there is a clear reason for speaking thus, if we consider the original Greek of the Prologue. You see, the Greek has two verbs corresponding to our verb 'be'. One verb, *einai*, corresponds to the being proper of God and may be translated as our verb 'be' in its various forms: am, is, was, etc. The other verb, *gynomai*, corresponds to the being proper of the creature and should be translated by some such phrase as 'come to be' (rather than 'become'). Following the strictest logic, then, the verb 'be' (*einai*) always goes with the Word (see verses 1.2.4.9.10), and the verb 'come to be' (*gynomai*) always goes with created things (see verses 3.6.10.12.13).

Grammar takes a leap here, however. The language of the creature somehow enters the essence of God. The correct translation of verse 14, usually given as 'the word became flesh', goes something like this. The term 'flesh' might better be translated as '(human) creature'. And the verb 'became' might better be translated 'came to be'. So we have:'The Word *came to be* (human) creature'. That is why I say that the Word divested itself of its divine attributes.[48]

As if that were not enough, the poetic language of the Prologue adds the phrase that spells out the human condition thus assumed: ". . . and pitched his tent among us" (v. 14). Of the verbs meaning 'dwell', the author of the Prologue chose the one most clearly indicating the contingent, transitory condition of humanity. Greek *skēnoun,* related to *skēnē* ('tent'), alludes to the tent of the nomad rather than the solid house of town and city dwellers. In other words, the divine essence revealed to us is a divine essence revealed in history, in the face of contingency and death.

This is further explicated in the rest of verse 14. It says: 'and we have seen his *glory* . . .', i.e., his divinity. If we ask where or how they saw it, we get a response that exempts us from looking for any manifestation or sign from heaven, or even the resurrection. Whether it be the *glory* of the Father or the corresponding *glory* of the Son reflecting that of the Father, it is the *glory* of one who is 'filled with grace and truth'.

These are the two great human qualities—goodness and fidelity to promises—that simultaneously and by the same process characterize the ideal of humanity and the ongoing response of God throughout the Old Testament. This is the real, true name that Moses was looking for (see Ex 34:6).

Moreover, we find that the rest of the fourth Gospel confirms our opinion that it is the human behavior of Jesus, not the suprahuman in him, that enables us to see his glory—or, what comes down to the same thing, to recognize his divinity. I readily grant that trying to solve problems posed by the Prologue by resorting to the rest of John's Gospel is not the most exegetically advisable method, since the two are probably independent. And especially if the Prologue is a hymn comparable to the two in Philippians and Colossians that Paul seems to cite in the second text we shall analyze along these lines further on. But on this point the Prologue and the rest of John's Gospel so clearly coincide that we can shore up our argument even more.

On two clear occasions John's Gospel indicates that this 'glorification', or visible manifestation of the 'glory' of Jesus, is realized before his death, and hence before his resurrection.[49] The second and most solemn (see Jn 1:13) takes place after such a lowly human and hardly divine seeming action as that of Jesus' washing of the feet of his disciples before dining with them for the last time (see Jn 13:31).

To this we should add a theological datum of great importance for John. A little later on the same occasion Philip asks Jesus to *show* them the Father. That will satisfy them. Then Jesus replies, or the theology of John's Gospel has him reply: "Who has seen me has seen the Father. How can you say, 'Show us the Father'?" (Jn 14:9). As if Jesus were saying: there is nothing to know about divinity in the Father that is not already present and visibly shown in what is human in me. The history in which they are present and involved shows *everything* that can be shown of the Father and his glory.

But it may well be Paul, even more than John, who plunges into this problematic issue of the coexistence of two natures in Jesus; logically enough, of course, he does not use such terms. This is appraised, above all, in the third stage of his letter-writing, in his letters from captivity. And he does so by apparently citing hymns referring to Christ that were already in existence.

If it were not anachronistic, we could say that the christological statement of the Letter to the Colossians, which calls Jesus the visible 'image of the invisible God' (Col 1:15), sums up what we have just seen in John's Gospel.[50] But we may properly ask: How can the *human* nature of Jesus be the full image of the Son's *divine* nature without losing its human characteristics? Wouldn't the divine be precisely that which surpasses the human seen in Jesus?

Unexpectedly and incredibly, Paul's reply is just the opposite. In his Letter to the Philippians, and again in a hymn to Christ, we find this assertion: "Who, being of *divine condition*, did not cling avidly to being equal to the divinity,[51] but *emptied* himself and took *the condition of a servant, coming to be* like human beings . . ." (Phil 2:6-7).

Note again the use of the verb 'come to be', which I have already discussed. I should also point out that the word translated above as 'condition' is more exactly 'form' (*morphē*). Its meaning may normally range from 'form' or 'appearance' to 'condition' or 'nature'. But the context supports the translation used above, since being a *servant* was not just the aspect adopted by Christ but also his real historical condition. For the same reason, and even with greater reason, we must realize that 'form' applied to the being of God can only mean God's *nature*—certainly not God's 'appearance' or 'aspect', given God's admitted 'invisibility'. It is just that Paul, perhaps more prudent than Chalcedon in his language, does not want to employ a term that commonly designates fixed and immutable elements. Hence our modern word 'condition' comes closer to the meaning that Paul intended to give to the word *morphē*.

Having noted these points, we may ask: What is Paul, or the hymn he cites, trying to say through this poetic language? To understand this, one would have to carry to a radical extreme the experience of 'acculturation' that we considered above, doing it out of love rather than out of mere curiosity, needless to say.

Let us take an imaginary example that might seem ridiculous, remembering some sort of parallel process must have gone on to arrive at the statement in the hymn cited by Paul. Let us imagine a passionate zoologist who sincerely and honestly wants to 'come to live' the existence of an ant. Let us imagine he possesses magical powers, but that he uses them in a way that is consistent with his original intention. What could or should he do?

First of all, it would be pointless for him to turn himself into just another ant and to cease forever being a human. If he did that, he would simply repeat the enigmatic existence of an ant in the very same way. The experiment would be lost, along with the experimenting subject.

Second, it would also be pointless for him to annul or abandon his human nature. For it is on the basis of that nature, with its specific world of values, that the experience takes on meaning and that the existence of the ant, without ceasing to be such, can be transcended and elevated.

Third, the experimenter's human nature would nevertheless have to be emptied of all those characteristics and conditions that are incompatible with an ant's life. Let us imagine that in this matter our freedom, or that of the zoologist, is total: that the 'form' of existing inherent as a *datum* in being human can be emptied, leaving only what freedom *wants to be* in terms of values. What is translated to the zoologist's existence in the *form* of an ant, then, is not his fixed, 'natural' characteristics of knowing, feeling, and acting but what constitutes his most authentic and original being.[52] To stay with biblical themes and terms, let us say that the human being would transfer to the existence of the ant his goodness (or graciousness) and fidelity,[53] emptying himself of the remaining 'human' features insofar as they were opposed to authentic 'ant' existence.

Some may say that this is nothing but foolish imagining. But what else is the whole biblical process, which shows us a God moving in this direction by offering God's very self to human understanding?

If Chalcedon did not incorporate these important and more imaginative elements to be found in John's Gospel and Paul's letters, if it left them out of its christological formula, the reason is, I think, that it was too bound to a philosophy that claimed to know the eternal, immutable divine nature. Chalcedon was ready to compromise or correct only those elements in that philosophy which seemed to contradict directly what had been manifested in Jesus. It did not possess any mental spare parts, perhaps because it was deliberately trying to get away from what it deemed merely poetic or insufficiently pure and metaphysical.

•

By way of summary, then, we can say that Chalcedon was trying to talk about the divinity of Jesus. In this attempt, and for want of anything better, it introduced a concept of the 'divine nature' that would give people the impression, especially with the passage of time, that it had canonized a philosophy (or metaphysics) that was actually incompatible with basic elements of its own formula and its most sound and well-balanced result: i.e., the 'linguistic communication' obtained, in Jesus, between history and the dimensions of the human being on the one hand and the way of expressing oneself about the divine on the other.

Thus later christologies, going against rather than along with the most crucial elements of the Chalcedon formula, would indulge in an ahistorical reading of Jesus of Nazareth. Here the 'divine nature' would exact its price. Christianity would show up more as just another religion among many than as the historical project to introduce the kingdom of God into the structures of this world.

As I see it, a serious consideration of christological problems will not end up declaring the Chalcedon formula obsolete. Instead it will show that we are far from having understood and appreciated all its richness and radicalness, much less implemented them theologically. That richness and radicalness undoubtedly remained implicit to some extent at the time; they were not fully perceived. But many christologies of our own day don't perceive them either.

This is particularly true with regard to a point that I should like to bring out here. If my above remarks are correct, then Chalcedon sets Jesus over against idolatry rather than atheism. Why do I say that? Am I trying to ingratiate myself with a certain class of readers? I don't think so, though I admit it is hard to plumb the basic mainspring of one's own motivation.

I don't think Chalcedon had atheism in mind for the obvious historical reason that atheism was not a social phenomenon of its time. Furthermore, Chalcedon did not decide and declare that Jesus is God. That had been done centuries earlier, and it already shows up in the writings of the New Testament. What Chalcedon adds by way of a more original contribution is that the process of 'divinizing' Jesus did not come down to first establishing the existence and characteristics of a divine realm and then ushering Jesus of Nazareth into them. If that had been the case, then the first and principal obstacle to the process would have been the human refusal to admit the existence of any such prior divine realm.

The process proposed and crowned by Chalcedon is the opposite: in his limited human history Jesus, interpreted from the standpoint of a centuries-old tradition seeking the meaning of human existence, shows us the Absolute, the ultimate reality, the transcendent datum *par excellence*. The thing being opposed, then, is first and foremost any and every absolutization of values other than those manifested by Jesus in his human history. The target, then, is the absolutization of what is false: i.e., idolatry.

Some might object here that atheism, by its negation of transcendence, is generically opposed to this datum: not because it takes any particular historical form or represents any particular set of values, but because it assumes and allows any such datum to be beyond the empirical and the verifiable.

Now if that were the primary, anthropological significance of atheism, I would have to agree that it represents an insurmountable obstacle to any possibility of being interested in the Jesus of Chalcedon. In Volume I, however, I sought to counter this mistaken notion by analyzing the meaning-structure of the human being. I sought to show that *any* human existence is structured by transcendent data. I urged that we revise a statement that is often taken for granted, and mistakenly so: i.e., that a person does not accept God because God transcends human experience.[54] And I suggested that we might ask ourselves whether people do not deny God, rather, because they see God as the sanction for *this or that specific* kind of human existence.

It is in that sense that the following pages of this volume may be of interest to atheists and Christians alike.

CHAPTER II

Christological Vacuum?
Praising, Reverencing, and Serving God

I

Sometimes the first christological datum that meets the eye in a programmed process of spirituality is the fact that various problems are resolved without the help, at least the visible help, of christology. Thus, it is a striking fact that in the Exercises, in the First Principle and Foundation specifically, the destiny of the human being and its existence in the world is decided without any apparent relation to christology.[55]

Before I explore the christological import of this conspicuous absence, however, let me mention several others that are just as obvious and that may contribute interesting data to our investigation. After the First Principle and Foundation, the whole First Week, devoted to meditation on sin, moves along without any explicit reference to any christological datum. Later we shall consider whether the colloquy of the first exercise really constitutes an exception. But even if we give that colloquy an importance greater than it has in the space dedicated to the exercises of the First Week, we are surprised by the difference between the First Week and the three following weeks, where Christ occupies an ongoing and central place. And after we have followed the stages in the life, death, and resurrection of Christ and approach the end of the Exercises, we are again surprised to find that the Contemplation to Attain the Love of God (230) is totally dissociated from any christology.

One more datum may help us in the overview. In the places lacking any explicit reference to Christ, we do not find some sort of vagueness or void. In every case the vacant spot, so to speak, is occupied by a consideration of God the Creator and his relation to the creature. The First Principle and Foundation, the First Week, and the Contemplation to Attain the Love of God: these three important moments of the Exercises are characterized by the continuing

41

invocation of 'God our Creator and Lord' and by frequent use of the word 'creature'.

Finally, to complete this overview, Ignatius also uses the Creator-creature terminology outside the process of the Exercises when he comments on the spiritual events taking place in them: e.g., in his Introductory Observations (5,15,16,20; *anotaciones* in Spanish). When he writes about Christ in them, Christ is merely an *object* of contemplation for the exercitant (4,19), not a *subject* communicating in some way with the exercitant. In this latter case, his language is constant and consistent. It is always a matter of the Creator and Lord who is at work in, and speaks to, his creature.

Now it is obvious that the absence of an explicit christology[56] is not by itself sufficient indication that no implicit christological elements exist in those key places either. That is a question to be studied and decided by careful analysis. It certainly should not be assumed *a priori*.

But neither should we assume *a priori* that the presence of christological elements in other places proves that there is an implicit christology to be found in the whole theological treatment of the Exercises: e.g., in the theological relationship between Creator and creature that is under consideration here. That question, too, must be examined in the light of the data. Only then can we see whether the remaining theological themes have been influenced by christology, and if so, by what sort of christology specifically.

I leave my readers in no doubt as to the result of my study of the First Principle and Foundation. It is wholly devoid of any christological influence. Not only does no explicit christology show up in it, but the Creator-creature relationship is wholly unaffected by any christology.

In this matter St. Ignatius is not an original or exceptional case. Indeed, the opposite would have been peculiar in his age. To some extent, indeed, the originality comes with the formulation of Vatican II in *Gaudium et spes* (n. 22), which tells us that Christ's revelation of the mystery of the Father and His love was at the same time a revelation of the mystery of the human being and its one, single, divine destiny.

One need only read the First Principle and Foundation to notice that its perspective is completely different. Its principal proposition is: "Man is created to praise, reverence, and serve God our Lord, and by this means to save his soul" (23). Here we have no indication of a mystery of love that is revealed only in Jesus Christ and that has to do with the Father's plans. The destiny of the human being is not so much a mystery as the consequence of a reasoning process, the premises of which are the nature of the Creator on the one hand and the nature of the creature on the other.

The crucial influence of philosophy, not of the christological mystery, on this formulation shows up equally but more subtly in the four attitudes that flow from the natural and supernatural relations between Creator and creature, according to the First Principle and Foundation. Since it did not go by way of the revelation of the Father's *mystery* and *love*, we find that the first two attitudes hint at an obvious dehumanization of the human being. They shall be our focus in the rest of this section.

Note that 'praising' and 'reverencing' are not *human* responses to a concrete love but the first *prehuman* consequences of the creature's discovery of its condition as creature, wherein human freedom plays no positive role. Note also that the word 'reverence' explicitly contains a central element of fear. And it could not be otherwise, if we limit ourselves to the terrifying impact of discovering the contingency of the creature and the transcendence of the Creator.

It may be useful to point out here that these two first attitudes belong properly to the final stages of Old Testament spirituality. They constitute what the Bible calls, in the positive sense, the religion of the 'flesh', i.e., of the creature. That might seem to contradict what I just said above about the 'philosophical' character of the First Principle and Foundation. I shall consider the matter further on. But it should be clear, even at this point, that in the age of Ignatius the central dividing line did not run between scholasticism[57] and the Old Testament but rather between both of them on the one hand and the New Testament—christology—on the other, although that opposition was not perceived.

It should not surprise us, then, to find that the First Principle and Foundation, and particularly the first two attitudes mentioned in it, are in open opposition to christological data such as those offered by Paul to the Romans and Galatians: "You did not receive a spirit of slavery, to fall back into fear again. You received a spirit of adoption as child, by which we cry out: Abba, Papa!" (Rom 8:15; Gal 4:3–6). It is obvious that this christological datum is definitely absent from the purpose of humanity as indicated in the First Principle and Foundation, at least insofar as the first two attitudes are concerned.[58]

Let us now move on to the third attitude, 'serving', and the sought-for result: 'and by this means to save his soul'.

II

After the obvious meaning of 'praising' and 'reverencing', we note that 'serving' introduces a certain ambiguity. It is true that the verb 'serve' is not the most appropriate one to indicate a fully human function, much less a divine one, such as that assumed to be the human vocation by the christology offered centuries later by *Gaudium et spes* (n. 22). On the one hand, *serve* could allude to a divine plan for history, a plan requiring the free, creative cooperation of the human being; and this vocation could also be called *service*. On the other hand, 'serve' can also mean mere obedience in fulfilling the orders of a master or lord, in this case the moral laws the Creator uses to test his creature.

Without fear of making a mistake, I can say that one of the major points in favor of Ignatius's theology, and one where he was most ahead of his age and its theology, is the fact that throughout the Exercises he more or less consistently maintained the *ambiguity* of the term 'serve' and its two possible meanings. But that should not obscure the fact that in the First Principle and Foundation it is the second meaning that is the obvious one: obedience in fulfilling the orders of a master or lord, obedience to a law. I offer four reasons to back up this assertion.

The *first* reason, certainly a central one, is that this service (or praise, reverence, and service, if you prefer) mentioned in the First Principle and Foundation is considered a *means* and not an end. It is not a *vocation* but an obligation imposing conditions on the goal envisioned: saving one's soul. Actually, we are not confronting something new or strange. We are in the presence of a conception that had been widely circulated since the Book of Wisdom, which views the existence of the human being as a *test*. Without detriment to God, we can say of this conception that the end sought by the human being does not really concern God but the human being itself. The goal is to pass the test successfully, to save one's soul. And the way to do that is to heed the orders or rules fixed by God (for the purpose of having some criterion of judgment). These rules operate automatically or mechanically in all other creatures, but not in the human being. The human being enjoys the dubious privilege of being required to offer free obedience, i.e., service.

I just noted above that one of the good points in Ignatius's theology, which would count for the future, was its maintenance of the ambiguity of the term 'service'. This enabled it to express the idea of a divine plan for history as well. But it must be pointed out that even in those passages where the latter meaning is clearer and more obvious, the former meaning does not disappear. Let us look at this in two key moments of the Exercises.

In the Call of an Earthly King, we find the notion of a universal plan in the two terms of the comparison: "It is my will to conquer all the lands of the infidel . . ." (93); "It is my will to conquer the whole world . . ." (95). Faced with this 'vocation', people should properly have two attitudes or resolves, according to Ignatius. One is to 'offer themselves entirely *for the work*'. The other is expressed this way by Ignatius: "Those who wish to give greater proof of their love and distinguish themselves in whatever concerns the *service* of the external King . . ." (97).

Here we do have a plan and a corresponding service. Nevertheless, the ambiguity remains if we look at more than one element. Note, first of all, that the purpose or aim behind this total service is not the plan itself, its intrinsic value, but 'distinguishing themselves'. Undoubtedly the reference is not to pride or haughtiness but to the competitive spirit of truly noble knights (94). On the other hand, the eternal King himself seems to put the reward above the intrinsic value of his plan. In short, we hear echoes of the First Principle and Foundation: ". . . and by this *means* to save his soul" (23). So, the eternal King wants to conquer the whole world, "and thus to enter into the glory of my Father. . . . Whoever wishes to join me . . . must be willing to labor with me, that by following me in suffering, he may follow me in glory" (95). Finally, we must keep in mind another reason that is implicit: the service to which the eternal King invites noble knights cannot be the goal or aim of all human beings. It can only be that of Christians, who are 'to conquer'; it cannot be that of those who are to be conquered (95).

The second key point in the Exercises where we find *service* associated with a plan is in the Three Kinds of Humility. Ignatius is very clear about the first kind of humility: "*This is necessary for salvation.* It consists in this, that as far as possible I so subject and humble myself as to *obey the law* of God our Lord in all things, so that not even were I made lord of all creation, or to save my life here on earth, would I consent to violate a commandment . . . that binds me under pain of mortal sin" (165).

In his discussion of the second kind of humility there is a point that is not clear, and it relates specifically to *service*: "I possess it if my attitude of mind is such that I neither desire nor am I inclined to have riches rather than poverty . . . provided only in either alternative I would *promote equally the service* of God our Lord and the salvation of my soul. Besides this indifference, this second kind of humility supposes that not for all creation, nor to save my life, would I consent to commit a venial sin" (166).

Two distinct criteria obviously interweave in this second kind of humility. One is the law, as in the first kind of humility, but at the higher level of avoiding venial as well as mortal sins. The other is the assumption that the matter at stake, where the first criterion is operative, is promoting *equally* the *service* of God. The logical explanation is that Ignatius is thinking here of the plan presented previously by the eternal King. For Ignatius, this 'conquering the world' always had a very concrete and practical sense. We can well imagine situations where there would be no difference in the options for carrying out the plan insofar as efficacy was concerned, except that one of the options would entail a venial sin.

This shows that the three kinds of humility are ordered to a *test*, which human beings can pass with a higher or lower grade. The essential 'service' asked of them is fulfillment of the law. To 'distinguish oneself' in that service is to accept that law, even with regard to the counsels of perfection that it explicitly or implicitly contains.

Furthermore, Christians live these exigencies of the test within a particular context: the service they can offer to the plan of the eternal King. But this service is an addition to the first, which is essential for the end of the human being, and it can never subsume that first service: obedience to the law. On these points, then, christology, even though present, does not ultimately manage to specify or determine the service that God asks of the human being, i.e., its destiny and purpose as a human being.

The *second* reason why I say that 'service', for all its ambiguity in Ignatius's vocabulary, does not allude to a general divine plan for human history stems from an examination of the way Ignatius treats the theme of *sin* in the First Week of the Exercises. This theme, too, is closely associated with the central lines of Ignatius's theology. Indeed it is likely that in its general and overall cast it represents a stage that is even earlier than the First Principle and Foundation.

Here again there is a certain ambiguity about the term 'service'. But here again, insofar as the end of the human being is concerned, the dominant meaning is that of a test; and the criterion is the fulfillment of the law preestablished by God in view of that test.

We get a typical indication of this conception in the first 'composition of place' for the first meditations on sins. In contrast with other contemplations where history provides the imaginative context (47), Ignatius here must *imagine* the human being in relation to sin without any more history than the person's condition as sinner: "In a case where the subject matter is not visible, as here in a meditation on sin, the representation will be to see in imagination my soul as a prisoner in this corruptible body, and to consider my whole composite being as an exile here on earth, cast out to live among brute beasts. I said my whole composite being, body and soul" (47).

I need hardly point out that in such a context service consistent with the image can only consist in a test. The image would be different if a divine plan were to be carried out in history. Note the passivity implied in such terms as 'prisoner' and 'exile'. Note the sensations of impotence and danger for the soul represented by the body and a mysterious 'animality' that may be either internal or external, i.e., alluding to one's own passions or temptations coming from the rest of humanity with its affairs and preoccupations. Everything seems to indicate that Ignatius wants to impress on the exercitant not only the 'test' situation he faces in life but also the seriousness and dangerousness of that test. Lest the familiar concerns of life and its usual purposes overwhelm this primordial concern, Ignatius insists that the exercitant use a different criterion of judgment: the law of God.

It would be time-consuming and unnecessary to examine all the elements that point in the same direction in the meditations on sins. I shall restrict myself to showing how the 'service' mentioned in the First Principle and Foundation is always framed within a test, where the criterion is not a historical plan of God but the fulfillment of an already established law that is the same for all.

Ignatius asks the exercitant to recall the sin of the angels: ". . . that they were created in the state of grace, that they did not want to make use of the freedom God gave them to reverence and obey their Creator and Lord . . ." (50). Note the limited function given to their freedom. It is reduced to reverence and obedience.

In meditating on the particular sin of every individual who went to hell for one mortal sin, one gets a heightened sense of the test involved and the unfairness of it. Its nature as a test, as opposed to collaboration in a divine plan for history, shows up clearly in the mere possibility that everything accomplished in a lifetime may be wiped out in an instant. The aspect of test is accentuated by the contrast between heaven or paradise on the one hand and hell on the other (50,51,71), these indicating the final end and purpose of human existence on earth. The unfairness of the test did not escape the attention of Ignatius when he was examining the case of those sent to hell for a single mortal sin. He makes an explicit effort to make sure that the exercitant understands why this should be so: "Use the understanding to consider that because of sin, and of acting against the Infinite Goodness, one is *justly* condemned forever" (52). The frailty of the human being and the mercifulness of God are thus separated from 'justice' in the strict sense, so that the aspect of test is made more pointed and acute. Indeed it is accentuated to the point where even less human instincts, such as fear, are enlisted in the struggle: ". . . that if because of my faults I forget the love of the eternal Lord, at least the fear of these punishments will keep me from falling into sin" (65).

Finally, in the meditation on one's own sins we are struck by the use of the category, beauty versus ugliness, to penetrate the nature of sin. After comparing myself with all other creatures and creation, and with God, "I will consider all the corruption and *loathsomeness* of my *body*; I will consider myself as a source of corruption and contagion from which has issued countless sins and evils and the most offensive poison" (58).

This use of the category of ugliness is really not so strange. For scholasticism, beauty, truth, and goodness were convergent and almost interchangeable attributes of being. Service is beautiful because good actions are in the service of God, the highest being. Hell, as the destiny opposed to God, has all the features of horror.

Sin must also be considered in terms of its metaphysical characteristics: "I will weigh the gravity of my sins, and see the loathsomeness [opposed to beauty] and malice [opposed to goodness] which every mortal sin I have committed has in itself, even though it were not forbidden" (57). We can see that service to the law of God with its commands and prohibitions is here more deeply grounded on the very nature of things and the relations differentiating creature from Creator, not on some plan that God might want to carry out and that is opposed by human refusal to collaborate in it. Thus, our sins break the order of the universe (60), not some plan of redemption, salvation, liberation, or whatever one might call it, that arises out of a christology.

There is a *third* reason why I claim that the 'service' indicated in the First Principle and Foundation does not allude to a divine historical plan but rather to obedience to God's commandments as a test involving human destiny. This reason is related to the argument just enunciated.

Right in the middle of the explicit christological absence of the First Week and its consideration of sin, we find the well-known 'colloquy' with the crucified Christ and its three famous questions: "What have I done for Christ? What am I doing for Christ? What ought I do for Christ?" (53).

Even more clearly than if Ignatius had used the word 'service' here, the idea of 'doing something for someone' eliminates all possible doubt as to whether service is being used in that sense here. He is clearly talking about setting to work to carry out the intention, plan, or project of another person—in this case, of Christ. I said earlier that Ignatius was theologically sound in maintaining the ambiguity of the term 'service'. Some readers might object that there is no such ambiguity here. Talk about what one has done for Christ can hardly be interpreted as mere obedience to the law of God.

That is true. But the ambiguity remains if we pay attention to the surrounding *context* of the colloquy, a context we have just been examining. It is a consideration of sin along the lines we have noted. Right away we must admit that the above colloquy cannot noticeably modify the total and detailed structure of the First Week, especially its theological orientation. Remember that with the exception of the fifth exercise on hell, which is an 'application of the senses', the other four exercises for the First Week are meditations with 'the three powers of the soul' (45). And it is in the process of 'applying the understanding by reasoning' (50) that we found the most certain and explicit data for determining Ignatius's conception of sin and its relationship or nonrelationship with possible data provided by christology. The colloquy with Christ is the first, and that is probably why Ignatius explains what a colloquy is and what we can expect from it: "The colloquy is made by speaking exactly as one friend speaks to another, or as a servant speaks to a master, now asking him for a favor, now blaming himself for some misdeed, now making known his affairs to him, and seeking advice in them" (54).

This description alone is enough to prove that we cannot derive any weighty argument from this colloquy to counter or relativize the arguments offered above. But there is more. Elements of this very same colloquy are intimately bound up with the notion of sin deriving from the sensation that we are *undergoing a test* in this world. And that, as we saw, is the key of the First Principle and Foundation.

As in other places where it is a matter of service (e.g., to the eternal King), stress is put more on a knightly conception than on the intrinsic value of some plan we should serve. The focus is not on the fact that our sin, our lack of due service, has obstructed the plan of Christ nailed to the cross. It is on the due 'shame and confusion' (48) I should feel when I compare what Christ did *for me* with my attitude toward him.

This is related to a fundamental element of the First Principle and Foundation: ". . . and by this means to save his soul" (23). In the colloquy under consideration here we are presented with Christ dying for our sins (53). In the second exercise on my own sins: "I will conclude with a colloquy, extolling the mercy of God our Lord, pouring out my thoughts to Him, and giving thanks to Him that up to this very moment He has granted *me* life. I will resolve with His grace to amend for the future" (61).

The second and last brief appearance of Christ in the First Week is in the meditation on hell, and specifically in a colloquy that is almost a meditation in itself. The exercitant is to call to mind those who are in hell, lost before, during, or after the coming of Christ: "Thereupon, I will give thanks to God our Lord that He has not put an end to *my* life and permitted *me* to fall into any of these three classes" (71).

The appearance of Christ in this colloquy does not seem to reflect any theological intention of giving thanks for the Father's divine providence. It has no evident theological reason at all. The purpose would seem to be, rather, to introduce greater concreteness into the moment of the colloquy. In any case, the exercitant does not thank Christ for the redemption of humanity or any universal plan, but merely for not having treated 'me' as others have been treated.

My point here is not to stress the cruelty of this notion of test. It is to recognize its presence once again, even when Christ explicitly appears in the First Week, and to note one of the most salient features it entails, a feature clearly opposed to service to some universal plan: i.e., individualism. *Every* individual human being is tested, and nothing can be done to alleviate this burden or rid another of it. And as the above texts also show, the outcome of the test depends on the human being, but most of all on the moment when God sends death (71; also 50,52,60).

A *fourth* and final reason for interpreting service as obedience to the law rather than as a call to become part of a historical plan is to be found in the key moment of the Exercises known as Making a Choice of a Way of Life (169–89).

It is important to note that in the introduction to this process Ignatius repeats the First Principle and Foundation almost word for word (169). This occurs only one other time, and specifically within the process of choosing a way of life (179). All the more important, then, are the following facts. Even after central meditations on Christ in the Exercises, there is no allusion to a divine plan nor a structural christological consequence for human freedom in these two passages. Indeed, even the key word under consideration here is missing: i.e., *service*. Note the following: "It is necessary to keep as my aim the end for which I am created, that is, the praise of God our Lord and the salvation of my soul. Besides this, I must be indifferent, without any inordinate attachment . . ." (179); "I must consider only the end for which I am created, that is, for the praise of God our Lord and for the salvation of my soul" (169). Readers must admit that the disappearance of the key word 'service', so readily used by Ignatius, in these two places cannot be dismissed as insignificant.

But there is more. Let us look at the most *reasoned* ways to choose a way of life, those that belong to the 'third time' of tranquillity (177). The core of the first way in this third time is "to weigh the matter by reckoning the number of advantages and benefits that would accrue to *me* if I had the proposed office or benefice solely for the praise of God our Lord and the salvation of *my soul*" (181). What might seem to be egotism here is nothing else but what we have already seen in the First Principle and Foundation. The criterion is clearly the praise of God within a conception of human life on earth as a test. But that criterion does not stem from any interest that God might have in our praise for historical purposes. Thus the praise of God, in the choice of a way of life as in the First Principle and Foundation, is a *means* to the essential end at stake in our test: the salvation of my soul.

The second way of choosing a way of life in time of tranquillity differs from the first only in that the exercitant imagines situations in which he or she would be more likely to follow the criterion that was central in the first way. Three situations are given: what I would advise a total stranger to choose for the greater glory of God and the greater perfection of his soul (185); what choice I would wish to have made at the hour of my death (186); what choice I would wish to have made if I were at the last judgment (187).

It has been pointed out[59] that the last two criteria indicate I should exclude from my deliberations all considerations having to do with the future. Both criteria, you see, agree in judging the matter in itself, without a future: either in the face of death or at the end of history when divine judgment takes place.

I think this opinion is exaggerated, but it cannot be denied that if discernment is confronted directly with death and God's absolute judgment, I am hardly encouraged to consider God's service, with its more or less foreseeable future projections, as the criterion behind my choice. Once again we find ourselves in a theological context dominated by the element of test. Bringing together the two moments when this test will be decided—personal judgment at death and universal judgment at the end of history—further reinforces its gravity in the mind of the exercitant.

By way of conclusion, then, let me repeat what I said at the very beginning of this chapter. It was not logical to expect Ignatius to provide a theology different from the one of his own age. The christological vacuum noticeable in his work is even more noticeable in contemporaries of his such as Calvin.[60] By the same token, however, it is not just a few words or expressions that point up this vacuum and that could and should fill it. It is the overall structure of the Excercises, in its mechanisms and key moments, that manifests a theology which is consistent in this respect.

But we have only begun our investigation.

CHAPTER III

Christological Vacuum?
Making Ourselves Indifferent

I

In the preceding chapter, I alluded to the passage in a document of Vatican II (GS:22) that tells us that only in the revelation of the Father and His love does Jesus Christ reveal to us the mystery of the human being and its divine destiny. The fundamental revelation of the Father can be put in the formula used twice in the First Letter of John to sum up what the witnesses heard, saw with their own eyes, and touched with their hands, regarding the Word of life (1 Jn 1:1): "God is love" (1 Jn 4:8.16). We cannot disdain the fact that no other place in the New Testament attempts a definition of sorts in this form: subject, verb 'be', predicate; and with these basic elements alone purports to define God as revealed in Jesus Christ.

Of course, it is possible in the abstract that the apparent predicate is the real subject, not the reverse, and hence that the term being defined is 'love', not 'God'. But no one could take this abstract possibility seriously, particularly in the light of the immediately surrounding context. As if that were not enough, the same letter tells us that "everyone who loves . . . knows God; whoever does not love does not know God . . ." (1 Jn 4:7-8). Hence it is clear that here, as in any definition, the unknown or poorly known thing is the subject (God), whereas the predicate (love) is known and thus provides knowledge of the subject.

So the human experience of love defines God. But what happens to a definition of this caliber? It turns out that philosophical thought, especially that deriving from Greek culture and later incorporated into the scholastic theology of the Middle Ages, assumed it had much more definite and precise knowledge of the term 'God' than of the term 'love'. So, without saying so, it defined love (in the Johannine statement at least) in terms of what it thought it knew about the essence of God.

The overall result of this long process of theology tied to philosophy was a

51

christological vacuum[61] in the very conception of God. The mystery of Christ did not reveal the mystery of the Father. It was kept outside it. Christology developed on its own. Christology was viewed in terms of those who believed in Christ and belonged to his Church. The human being *as such* was directed to a more metaphysical than christological conception of God insofar as its destiny and vocation were concerned.

Now let us stop and go back to the First Principle and Foundation of the Ignatian Exercises. In the previous chapter we looked at the first three attitudes implied in the Ignatian theology of the Creator-creature relationship and its relation, or lack of relation, to christology. Those three attitudes were: praise, reverence, and service vis-à-vis God.

But there remains a fourth attitude of substantive importance: *indifference.* Now it might seem obviously contradictory that God is love but that we human beings "must make ourselves indifferent" (23). The problem is not that simple. There is indeed a real problem here, as we shall see, but it does not lie merely in the opposition between two apparently contradictory attitudes.

To begin with, love and indifference are not *reciprocal* attitudes. In other words, it is not a matter of responding to God's love with human indifference. The First Principle and Foundation presents indifference in connection with all created things, i.e., with everything that is not God. It might almost be viewed as a precondition for responding unreservedly to God's love.

Let us read the rest of the First Principle and Foundation: "The other things on the face of the earth are created for man to help him in attaining the end for which he is created"(23). That end being "to praise, reverence, and serve God our Lord, and by this means to save his soul" (23). In terms of this end, then, the existence and subordination of other creatures means that "man is to make use of them in as far as they help him in the attainment of his end, and he must rid himself of them in as far as they prove a hindrance to him." And if this criterion is to be perfectly observed in practice, a fourth attitude is necessary: "*Therefore, we must make ourselves indifferent to all created things.*" What is commanded or prohibited by God is obviously excepted from this norm. To exemplify the area where indifference is in order, Ignatius writes: "Consequently, as far as we are concerned, we should not prefer health to sickness, riches to poverty, honor to dishonor, a long life to a short life. . . . Our one desire and choice should be what is more conducive to the end for which we are created" (23).

Two things attract our attention in this logic, which has been called 'one of the most perfect models' of scholastic speculation.

The first thing is that the indifference under discussion here is no more nor less than desiring and choosing 'what is more conducive to the end for which we are created'. Contrary to what it might seem to be at first glance, making ourselves indifferent does not mean putting an end to all desire but transferring our desire from any given created thing whatsoever to that which appears to reason to be the most conducive to our end. So *reason, desire, and choice,* in that order, are the three logical moments in the use of liberty or freedom in the created.

In an excellent study of concupiscence, Karl Rahner has shown that this seeming but impossible victory over concupiscence ('inordinate attachment' in Ignatius's terminology) would really be fatal to any well-balanced anthropological conception; and that—here is the christological datum—such an ordering cannot be conceived even in Christ.[62]

Leaving aside that important issue for the moment, let us examine the second thing that attracts our attention in the logic and formulas of the Exercises as cited above. It is the sense or point of the limitation that the First Principle and Foundation sets on indifference. We are to make ourselves indifferent to created things, 'as far as we are allowed free choice and are not under any prohibition' (23). It applies, then, to what are called '*indifferent* actions' in classical moral theology.

What is not clear here is the reason for the limitation. *Total* indifference would be more logical. As I gradually found out what was permitted and forbidden to me by the law, I would then not feel the least desire contrary to that law, the fulfillment of which, reason tells me, is conducive to the salvation of my soul.

It is important to note here the relationship between indifference and a central theme of the Exercises that is brought up in the very first Introductory Observation, which explains the nature of the Exercises: ". . . so we call Spiritual Exercises every way of preparing and disposing the soul to rid itself of all inordinate attachments" (1).

Now the fact is that I am commanded to 'honor thy father and thy mother'. Obviously, I cannot be indifferent to those 'creatures' because this is not an area where 'indifference' is in force. But since love for father and mother can *become* inordinate at any given moment, it would seem safer to carry indifference into the realm of the law itself because it is not possible to begin it at a given point of 'attachment'. At some places in the Exercises, then, the notion of a certain limit and of anthropological balance gets lost. In the third exercise of the First Week we note these graded requests in the colloquy: "1. A deep knowledge of my sins and a feeling of abhorrence for them; 2. An understanding of the *disorder* of my actions, that filled with horror of them, I may amend my life and put it in order; 3. A knowledge of the world, that filled with horror, I may put away from me all that is worldly and vain" (63).

It is clear that the third point is intimately connected with indifference; but, as in the *Imitation of Christ and Despising of the World*, the logic is carried to the extreme of abhorring or despising the world. One might claim that by 'world' here Ignatius is alluding to inordinate attachments themselves; in that case, however, the gradation of the colloquy, already obvious in the second point, would be lost. If, on the other hand, the law of God presupposes 'ordered' attachments to it, then 'indifference' would come down to having no attachment until reason told me whether and to what extent a certain thing was in accord with God's law; but that would lead to the serious anthropological error studied by Karl Rahner in his article on concupiscence.

The obvious response that Ignatius should have prepared for this problem would be that I *already* know what is commanded and prohibited and therefore have a clear picture of what I ought to desire and have no need of indifference. But such is not the case anyway. No matter how well I may know by heart and understand the ten commandments, their reach and scope in the various new and complicated circumstances of real life remain unknown to me—unless I happen to be one of those classic experts in moral theology, and even then . . .

Hence the zone of indifference would have to be amplified to make room for everything about which I am unsure whether it is commanded or prohibited. And that is not all, if we take as an example an ancient Israelite confronting the decalog. Since certain commandments have notorious exceptions, we realize that our Israelite should, strictly speaking, become indifferent to killing or not killing. For the commandment, 'Thou shalt not kill', was restricted by count-less occasions where killing became an obligation.

So, step by step, we have come to the heart of the problem: How does the law move from the most abstract and general formulas to concrete commands and prohibitions that do not figure in those formulas?

Biblical theology answered this question by showing how this transition was made by the *prophets* and by Jesus himself. The central criterion for grasping the further reach of the law is God's *preference*—i.e., God's nonindifference—because the law itself, in its very normative purpose, is a sign of that prefer-ence. The commandment, 'Thou shalt not kill', is not the result of a comparison between the number of times one has to say 'no' and the number of times one should say 'yes'; it is God's determined preference for the long life of the human being. Thus, after the commandment to honor father and mother, Deuteronomy adds: ". . . that you may have long life and prosper in the land that Yahweh your God is giving you" (Dt 5:16). In other words, the nonindif-ference of Yahweh regarding a *long or short life* explains the law, permitting people to fulfill it and apply it to circumstances that were not foreseen in its formulation.

In like manner, Jesus' nonindifference toward the *poverty* inflicted on the masses of Israel is translated into his blessing of the poor, his preferential treatment of them, his different way of viewing the gravity of their sins, and hence even the obligation to share one's riches with them in order to attain eternal life, something that does not show up in any law (Mt 19:16-24).

Hence we may rightly question the logic of conceiving this zone of indiffer-ence, from the moral standpoint, as an area where 'indifference' to created things would be the most rational attitude. And we might also note in passing that it is christology which, by speaking to us more clearly about the 'prefer-ences' of God (who is love) and God's plan to make them effective in history, raises serious doubts about the correctness of 'making ourselves indifferent' in order to better achieve the end for which human beings were created.

II

The logic of indifference has not yet spoken its last words, which are two. The first is that indifference is merely the 'foundation' for a preference whereby Christ himself made his preference and choice. It has always been understood, and rightly, that the Three Kinds of Humility (165–68) are the continuation and development of the First Principle and Foundation. They are a further step forward, a preference which finds its inspiration in Jesus: ". . . whenever the praise and glory of the Divine Majesty would be equally served, in order to imitate and be in reality more like Christ our Lord, I *desire and choose* poverty with Christ poor, *rather than* riches; insults with Christ loaded with them, *rather than* honors; I desire to be accounted as worthless and a fool for Christ, *rather than* to be esteemed as wise and prudent in this world. So Christ was treated before me" (167).

As we shall have occasion to see more fully in the next chapter, indifference becomes a desire and preference, the object of which is the imitation of Christ. But does that bring us to something that is properly christological?

We must not overlook the fact that the shift from *indifference* in the First Principle and Foundation to *preference* in the third kind of humility is really prepared by the strategic meditation on the Three Classes of Men 'to choose that which is better' (149).

The first two classes are simple but superb psychological observations on how attachment to things distorts people's judgment about them and hence their choice of a way of life.

We are interested here in the third class because only there do we read about indifference and the means to achieve it in practice, to '*make ourselves* indifferent', as the First Principle and Foundation puts it.

The third class is made up of people who "want to rid themselves of the attachment [to something acquired not entirely as they should have, for the love of God (150), in order to find peace in God our Lord (153)], but they wish to do so in such a way that *they desire neither to retain nor to relinquish* the sum acquired. They seek only to will and not will *as* God our Lord inspires them . . ." (155).

Ignatius proposes two psychological means of arriving at this 'indifference', for that is what he is talking about in somewhat different terms. The first means is this: "Meanwhile, they will strive to conduct themselves as if every attachment to it had been broken [Segundo: as if they had broken with it in effect[63]]. They will make efforts neither to want that, nor anything else, unless the service of God our Lord alone moves them to do so. As a result, the *desire to be better able to serve God our Lord* will be the cause of their accepting anything or relinquishing it" (155).

The second means completes the first in the same general line, especially if we take the reading 'effect' rather than 'affect' or 'attachment' in the preceding passage: "It will be very helpful in order to overcome the inordinate attachment, even though corrupt nature rebel against it, to beg our Lord in the colloquies to *choose us* to serve Him in actual poverty. We should insist that we desire it, beg for it, plead for it, provided, of course, that it be for the *service* and *praise* of the Divine Goodness" (157).

This description is the most concrete description of the path to indifference in the Exercises, and it is here that the difficulties show up most clearly. At first glance we may think they are of a psychological nature; but, in fact, they ultimately point up the christological vacuum we have been encountering at every stage of our investigation.

In the first passage cited above, we have a person who has acquired a created thing, a sum of money, because of the attachment he has for it. This attachment is not associated with loving, serving, or praising God, but neither does it constitute a sin. Thus, it is what Ignatius would call an 'inordinate attachment', since it is not ordered in accordance with the criteria of the First Principle and Foundation. The 'disordered' nature of the attachment is also brought out by the fact that it somehow prevents the possessor from finding 'peace in God our Lord' (153). He is afraid that any attempt to draw closer to God will mean the loss of the thing he possesses.

I might note quickly in passing that there is a problem with Ignatius's grammar in one passage cited above. He uses an indicative where a subjunctive would make more sense and avoid a contradiction in his description of the third class (155). That subjunctive sense is brought out clearly in the English text used here, so we need not dwell on the point: "These want to rid themselves of the attachment, but they wish to do so in such a way that they desire neither to retain nor to relinquish the sum acquired" (155). In other words, they want to move from inordinate attachment to nonattachment, i.e., to indifference.

What about the mechanics of this indifference? It clearly seems to be a matter of fighting an inordinate attachment with its opposite, so as to arrive at a balance that will constitute indifference. Since the starting point in this case is an inordinate attachment to the sum of money acquired and a desire to keep it, the procedure would be to abandon it effectively or affectively, or to ponder doing so for as long as the will of God remains unclear. Moreover, in the colloquy we ask God to let us do this by showing us that it is his will.

Here we undoubtedly have an example of the well-known procedure of 'acting against' (*agere contra*, 97). We correct an inordinate attachment by choosing its opposite. It is akin to burning one's bridges, although not completely.

I say 'not completely' because that would be contrary to indifference. In such a case we would simply be replacing one inordinate attachment with another equally inordinate attachment, even though the latter might be heroic. When we are dealing with indifference, we are dealing with an area where commands and prohibitions are not operative. It is an area open to manifestations of God's will and, in many instances, of changes in that will.

Herein lies the difficulty. Either that strategy is ineffective, at most reducing the inordinateness of the attachment a bit; or else it can drag the whole person in an entirely new direction. Thomas Clancy tells us about a young Jesuit who decided to do something great for God when he was in high school. It was the 1950s, and doing something great for God meant doing something painful and difficult. Since the most painful thing he could envision was becoming a priest, he decided to become a priest. The most arduous road to the priesthood was that of the Jesuits, he felt, so he decided to become a Jesuit. When he entered the Jesuits, the life of a missionary was considered the most demanding; so he decided to become a missionary. Finally, after some years in the missions, he realized that he was not happy at all.[64]

If we take the final assessment as synonymous with 'not finding peace in God our Lord', then we will find in this case a proof that this was not the way to 'rid oneself' of an inordinate attachment; or, at the very least, we will find material for our reflection on the mechanism or procedure indicated.

It is clear that Ignatius is not claiming that indifference is a *state*, a general attitude of lack of interest in created things and life bound up with them. Indifference is not the absence of attachment; it is attachment liberated from the power of things, from the disorder introduced by their power. It is obviously a matter of transferring our attachment from the created thing to the value-criterion that should govern our decision to take it or leave it. Thus, at a first level, every attachment to what is commanded of me—no matter how great that attachment may be—and the consequent detachment from what is forbidden to me are ordered attachments.

The problem begins, as we saw earlier, when we realize that it is impossible for us to feel affection or attachment for an abstract principle. The things commanded or prohibited by God are not decisions made at random by his will; they are *preferences* for those things beneficial to human beings. It hardly seems possible to work up enthusiasm for God's commandment not to kill if we dissociate it from God's preference for a long life over a short life, that preference undoubtedly being the basis for the commandment. The same would apply to the commandment not to bear false witness and God's preference for honor.

Whatever be the case in this first area and preference for its abstract criterion—the fact that it is the law of God—we see here, as in the three degrees of kinds of humility, that there is a broad area of things or creatures not covered under any law. And we note that the first two classes show us how attachment to things sidetracks our chances of making a 'good choice' (169) and how we are to combat that sort of attachment.

But let us assume for a moment that the attachment is the very opposite of the one noted by Ignatius in discussing the classes of men. For whatever reason, a person could be inclined by attachment to give up his economic assets or a good portion of them. Nothing in the law of God, obviously, commands or prohibits this; and if this should be our own case, then we are obviously 'not indifferent to poverty and riches' (157). Should we then follow the logic of Ignatius through and say in this case: "It will be very helpful in order to overcome the inordinate attachment . . . to beg our Lord in the colloquies to choose us to serve Him in actual wealth. We should insist that we desire it, beg for it, plead for it, provided, of course, that it be for the service and praise of the Divine Goodness"?

Anyone experienced with the Exercises will see clearly that the answer to this question is 'no'. But it will not prove so easy to explain the logic behind that answer.

Not only in the First Principle and Foundation but also in the meditation on the Three Classes of Men, Ignatius clearly states that it is a matter of being 'indifferent to poverty and wealth' (23,157). It turns out, however, that only attachment to wealth is inordinate. It seems that the indifference to both poverty and wealth, the lack of preference for *either* this *or* that, as stipulated in the First Principle and Foundation, no longer holds.

This logical inconsistency leads us to recognize that, aside from the commanded and the prohibited, there is *another criterion*, an implicit one, to which our attachment should adhere and before which even indifference is inappropriate. What is this criterion?

It will not be difficult to find it. But in the Second Week, which is devoted to the contemplation of Christ, we will be surprised to find that its expression is, in many if not most cases, very much linked up with our creaturely condition.

Thus, in no less a place than the Call of an Earthly King, we are shown that indifference in the realm of the permitted bows to a loftier preference: "Those who wish to give greater proof of their love, and to distinguish themselves in whatever concerns the service of the eternal King and the Lord of all, will not only offer themselves entirely for the work, but will *act against their sensuality and carnal and worldly love*, and make offerings of greater value and of more importance . . ." (97).

This means that even in the zone where the law is not operative, indifference, properly speaking, does not occur except, at most, as a stage for a preference marked by the criterion involving the three great *enemies* of the human being (or the soul): the world, the flesh, and the Devil. So it definitely is *not* a matter of doing what is suggested in the First Principle and Foundation, of making ourselves 'indifferent' to all created things as far as we are allowed free choice and are not under any prohibition, of *not preferring* health to sickness, *riches to poverty, honor to dishonor*, a long life to a short life, and so on with all other things (23).

Nor is it correct, as we have seen, that in this area (170,178): "I must be indifferent, without any inordinate attachment, so that I am not more inclined or disposed to *accept the object in question than to relinquish it, nor to give it up than to accept it*. I should be like a balance at equilibrium, without leaning to either side . . ." (179).

Such is not the case, we now realize, because when it comes to creatures, accepting and relinquishing are not the same, once we take due account of sensuality, the world, and the flesh. Thus, "when we feel an attachment opposed to *actual poverty* or a repugnance to it, when we are not *indifferent to poverty and riches*, it will be very helpful in order to overcome the inordinate attachment, even though corrupt nature [*la carne*] rebel against it, to beg our Lord in the colloquies to choose us to serve Him in actual poverty" (157). But this observation obviously does not hold true for someone who feels an attachment opposed to wealth or a repugnance to wealth! And the reason is that a repugnance to wealth presumably cannot derive from 'the *flesh*'.

I noted above that the preference, which banishes any presumed indifference in the realm of the licit, is based on the notion of the enemies confronting humanity and the soul: the world, the flesh, and the Devil. It is not precisely a christological notion. Yet, curiously enough, it is the content of a key meditation in the Excercises that seems to be christological: the Meditation on Two Standards. In it the Devil, the third enemy and 'the enemy of our human nature' (135), proposes his plan for the demons: "First they are to tempt them to covet *riches* . . . that they may more easily attain the empty honors of this world, and then come to overweening pride. . . . From these three steps the evil one leads to all other vices" (142).

It may well be even more significant that Jesus, to counter this plan of the Devil, does not propose a historical plan but imitation of himself (147) in order to 'lead men to all other virtues' (146).

Some readers may say that here at least we cannot talk about a 'christological vacuum'. Why? Because the 'imitation' of Christ becomes a central theme of the whole week and, as we have seen, an *explicit criterion of preference* in the major meditation on the Three Kinds of Humility (167).

But that reply might be just a bit too facile. Let me point up two elements. The first, the importance of which will be examined more closely in the next chapter, is the fact that we are faced with a very peculiar christology, even though it was common at the time: i.e., the *imitation* of Christ combined with the *despising of the world*. In other words, the example of Jesus converges with a view of the human creature as besieged by its enemies. I would say that it does not go beyond a consideration, albeit a profound consideration, of the Creator-creature in the world relationship.

Christ incarnates a principle that does away with indifference in the realm of the licit, putting preference in a more secure but more abstract criterion. That principle is expressed clearly and succinctly at the end of Directions for the Amendment and Reformation of One's Way of Living in His State of Life: "Every one must keep in mind that in all that concerns the spiritual life his progress will be in proportion to his *surrender of self-love and of his own will and interests*" (189).

The second element is of even greater christological importance, however, because it again poses the problem of indifference vis-à-vis Christ. It turns out, you see, that the imitation of Christ is not the *ultimate criterion* for choosing in the realm of the licit. The strange fact is that an objective evaluation of what is better, endorsed by nothing less than the testimony of the life and death of the Son of God, takes a back seat to another criterion. And this other criterion should keep us indifferent to the very example of Christ himself until we discover how it is applicable to our own lives.

In the offering that terminates the Call of an Earthly King we read: "I protest that it is my earnest desire and my deliberate choice . . . to imitate Thee in bearing all wrongs and all abuse [dishonor] and all poverty, both actual and spiritual . . ." (98). But two limitations are added that logically suppose a certain indifference: . . . "*provided only it is for Thy greater service and praise*" and "*should* Thy most holy majesty *deign to choose and admit me* to such a state and way of life" (98). These are obviously conditional clauses.

The same thing occurs in the Meditation on Two Standards. In the colloquy addressed to Mary, we ask to be received under her Son's standard "in the highest spiritual poverty, and *should* the Divine Majesty be pleased thereby, and *deign to choose* and accept me, even in actual poverty . . ." (147). We find the same thing in the Three Classes of Men (155), most clearly in its concluding Note: "It will be very helpful in order to overcome the inordinate attachment, even though corrupt nature [*la carne*] rebel against it, to beg our Lord in the colloquies to choose us to serve Him in actual poverty. We should insist that we desire it, beg for it, plead for it, *provided, of course, that it be for the service and praise of the Divine Goodness*" (157).

Finally, we find this same criterion dominating everything, including the imitation of Christ, in the key to choosing a way of life that is embodied in the Three Kinds of Humility. We are told that the third kind of humility "is the most perfect kind of humility. It consists in this. If we suppose the first and second kind attained, then *whenever the praise and glory of the Divine Majesty would be equally served*, in order to imitate and be in reality more like Christ our Lord, I desire and choose poverty with Christ poor, rather than riches . . ." (167).

What are we to make of a praise and glory of God, the end of the human being, that could be *equal* with greater or lesser imitation of Christ, or, as other passages suggest, that could be greater without the highest degree of imitation?

The christological vacuum again appears inexorably right in the middle of the Second Week, indeed at the culminating point of the Exercises: the Choice of a Way of Life.

The only plausible explanation is that the general criterion must be subordinated to the personal vocation that the Creator appoints for his creature. But that entails two consequences that are not very easy to accept.

The first is this. Contrary to what is said in the Three Kinds of Humility, indifference should persist even after seeing what the most loyal imitation of Jesus Christ our Lord means. Otherwise, my investigation of what God wills *for me* will be prejudiced by a bias or preference.

The second consequence is of greater theological importance. After all the *objective* criteria studied, the only criterion that remains for me to know whether God does or does not will the extreme imitation of Christ for me is the *subjective* criterion of spiritual movements or experiences (175) and of those times "when much light and understanding are derived through experience of desolations and consolations and discernment of spirits" (176). I am not going to debate the validity of this method here. I will simply point out that it is not christological. Its envisioned aim is "that the Creator and Lord in person communicate Himself to the devout soul . . . and dispose it for the way in which it could better serve God in the future" (15).

It is worth noting here that the new element introduced by Christ in the area of *desire* has the same characteristics we saw in the area of *service* in the previous chapter. There is no unification of the two criteria. In other words: consideration of Christ—the christological element—introduces a *distinct* criterion; but it is not yet the *definitive* one.

Such is the case in the Exercises, despite the fact that a mere glance at the Old Testament could have made clear those preferences: present in the intrinsic value of things commanded and prohibited by the law, and even more clearly present when the prophets, like Deuteronomy, link up the proper attitudes of the human being with a divine plan for Israel and the whole of humanity.

The fact is that the logical basis of the indifference demanded by Ignatius is the indifference displayed by God in establishing the law and then some more personal tests of service. That indifference dovetails precisely and necessarily with a human existence viewed as a *test*. We saw that in the previous chapter and we run into it again here. In other words: the laws of God and subsequent personal vocations do not find their intrinsic intelligibility in any historical plan revealed in and through Christ. They have been set up to test the human being.

III

In two chapters, then, we have come across the same logic. We have seen it in our analysis of the First Principle and Foundation and in our consideration of its further derivations in the rest of the Exercises. So it is time to offer a historical and theological explanation of this conception.

I noted that the result of Christ's revelation could be summed up in the assertion that God is love. But instead of starting from the experience of love in order to understand God, philosophy, believing it already knew what God was, actually defined what *love* could be by taking it as the predicate or complement of a sentence in which God was the subject and the verb was a form of 'be'. The view resulting from such a philosophy or theology is well described by Schubert Ogden:

> In a similar way, supernaturalists have traditionally maintained that the end of man is to serve or glorify God through obedience to his will and commandments. And yet the God whom we are thus summoned to serve is, in the last analysis, so conceived that he can be as little affected by our best actions as by our worst. As *actus purus*, and thus a statically complete perfection incapable in any respect of further self-realization, God can be neither increased nor diminished by what we do, and our action, like our suffering, must be in the strictest sense wholly *indifferent* [Segundo italics] to him.[65]

It is not without reason that Ignatius wittingly or unwittingly avails himself of a theological stratagem in the First Week. In the colloquy he presents the crucified Jesus, not God under any guise whatever. Why? Not because Jesus is more 'imaginable' than the Father but because Jesus, in his human nature, suffered the consequences of our sins; and the assumption is that Jesus, in his divine nature, was and ever remains indifferent to them.

The fact that God is love, then, must be explained in a different way. Ignatius relates it exclusively to the activity of God in creation, whereby I receive everything that I am. It is thus not so strange or surprising that the Contemplation to Attain the Love of God concludes the Exercises by provoking my response to the *creative* love of God. For that is really the only way that God has, "*as far as He can*, to give Himself to me according to His divine decrees" (234).

God decides to create a free human being while he himself remains infinite, immutable, and happy. This God can only offer human beings the strange love of a chance to prove themselves in a test. If they pass the test, they gain salvation, a share in the divine life.

We need not assume that Ignatius was especially knowledgeable about scholastic philosophy just because his Exercises bear such clear traces of that conception, both in its handling of the final end of the human being and its immediate consequence: i.e., indifference. I say that for several reasons.

First, theology's treatment of God had followed this course for centuries, letting christology show another face of God but without thereby altering the first face. Thus, even though it is certain that Christ, the Son of God, died on the cross for humanity, God can *decide* to send death to a human being after his or her first mortal sin and thus assign that human being to hell for all eternity. And it definitely is a matter of *deciding*, as we see in the meditation on sins. In discussing those who have gone to hell, it blandly refers to "*countless others who have been lost for fewer sins than I have committed*" (52). That this is not accidental is evident from the fact that I must give thanks for it.

Second, Scripture itself, especially in those texts most influenced by Greek philosophical thought, already presents the destiny of the human being as a test (Wis 3:5). Along with this goes a characteristic spirituality, which seems to be present in some parts of the New Testament and which certainly continued to have an influence after that time.[66]

In the Book of Wisdom (Chapters 1–5), human beings seem to be divided into two groups. One group is made up of people who believe in justice and stake their lives on the wager that justice and righteousness will win out over death. They believe, in other words, that the fulfillment of the law has a value that death itself cannot destroy. For the first time in the Bible, we find here the explicit belief in a universal judgment after death, where the puzzle will be solved, where appropriate rewards and punishments will be meted out as they have not been here in human history. The other group of people does not share these beliefs at all.

What interests us here is the logic, the respective conduct, that these two different wagers introduce into the lives of the people in the two groups. The consequence of not believing that justice survives death is moral indifference to the means that might be used to accumulate satisfactions here on earth, as many and as intense as possible. Believing in the definitive victory of justice, on the other hand, entails a reserve and a patience that will see its fruit only in the future. This earthly world and its results must be ceded to those who adopt the principle: "Let our might be the norm of justice" (Wis 2:11).

Now it is not easy for people to spend their lives contemplating the 'results' of those who specialize in earthly success by any and every means. And since just, upright people are also busy, laboring and struggling for accomplishments compatible with the law, the inner logic of the Book of Wisdom clearly, though perhaps implicitly, consists in indifference to any and every result except the final one. Any enthusiasm for the acquisition of a value, even a licit one, entails a tremendous risk: the danger of forgetting that we are in a test situation, and the temptation to emulate those who do not worry about the rightness of the means but only about their efficacy.

We find a clear reflection of this picture of human nature, still surviving, in the Christian era. We are told that the anchorites, obliged by the law of God to work for a certain number of hours, used to undo at night the mats they had made during the day—so as not to be tempted by the *results* of their actions.

Now the opposite of valuing *results* in history is valuing merits. Calculating merit and what is meritorious is a characteristic feature of the Exercises (14,33,40,44). Perhaps the passage that most clearly displays this indifference to results, and the consequent valuation of merit, is this one in the General Examination of Conscience: "There are two ways of *meriting* from evil thoughts that come from without. . . . 2. When the same evil thought comes to me, and I *resist* it, but it returns again and again, and I always resist it till it is conquered. This second way is *more meritorious* than the first" (33–34). Obviously, this ongoing struggle has no use whatever for achieving any historical result, not even in terms of good works. It is clearly tied to the conception of human life as a test, in which one strives to 'distinguish oneself' (97).

So we see that indifference, as the consequence of a specific idea of human destiny, threads its logical way through the Spiritual Exercises to the very end. It is viewed as the most consistent and safe attitude for the test situation that is human life on earth.

Shaped in the Spiritual Exercises of Ignatius, Pierre Teilhard de Chardin explored the problem thoroughly in *The Divine Milieu*.[67] He never referred explicitly to the Exercises in that book, but he writes eloquently of the dehumanization introduced by that sort of indifference to the results of human activity in the realm of the licit. His remarks clearly bring out that such a conception of human beings and their lives, as involved in a test situation, is untenable in the face of the central data of christology.

But it is precisely this function of christology, i.e., showing how God is preparing the kingdom and introducing it into history, that is missing in any conception dominated by the notion of test and its criterion, the law.[68]

CHAPTER IV

The Christology Underlying the Imitation of Christ

I

In the two previous chapters we have seen that properly christological elements and criteria show up belatedly in the Exercises, and that they are superseded by other theological criteria at crucial and essential points in the Exercises. In short, despite all appearances the Ignatian Exercises are more theocentric than christological. And even that might not have been such a serious problem if the theocentric element in the Exercises had been shaped, as it should have been, by the revelation of the Father offered to us by the Son.

It should be clear now to my readers that my hypothesis about a christological vacuum does not depend on the statistical number of times that the Exercises allude to God or Christ. I said, for example, that the first christological element shows up in the colloquy associated with meditation on the three sins (53) in the First Week. But we must remember that this colloquy, as Ignatius himself tells us, is to be made at midnight of the very day when the exercitant begins the Exercises,[69] although one has to get through a fair number of pages in the Exercises to reach it. From the standpoint of material content, moreover, from the very start of the Second Week to the final contemplation exclusively, *all* the Exercises become an ongoing contemplation of the life, death, and resurrection of Jesus of Nazareth. The First Week deals with the purgative way, and the other three weeks are connected with the illuminative and unitive ways; but, in the mind of Ignatius, their division is in accordance with the mysteries of Christ's life that are contemplated in them (10,4).

Thus, it is not easy to characterize the theology present in the Exercises by noting only the content of those contemplations. Ignatius himself advises the director to 'narrate accurately the facts' (2), which are always taken literally from the text of one evangelist or from some harmonized version of several gospel texts. In doing this, Ignatius never displays the slightest suspicion that each evangelist represents a specific 'christology' or a distinctive interpretation of Christ, not even in the rather obvious case of the fourth Gospel.

Moreover, it would be anachronistic of us to assume that in his day Ignatius could have been aware of different christological currents within the Catholic Church, much less within the New Testament. It was not a widely discussed and debated topic, as other topics were. Ignatius and others lived in tranquil fidelity to the christological dogmas that had been established in the first few centuries, especially at Nicea and Chalcedon.

That does not mean that the christology present in the Exercises is vague, obscure, or incapable of being analyzed. It means, first of all, that we must look for its peculiar nature in accents or interpretations that Ignatius himself gives to his spirituality. In the Exercises we find them in notes and asides, or in certain particular contemplations that are in the nature of parables invented by Ignatius himself.

Second, it also means that if we are going to describe the christology of the Exercises in terms of categories and labels belonging to the last few centuries,[70] then we must be careful to acknowledge the relativity of all such classifications. We do better to point up the influence of different conceptions of Christ on the spirituality associated with them, the spirituality of the Ignatian Exercises in this case.

By the same token, however, we cannot ignore the fact that the spirituality of Ignatius continues to be operative today. It is about that still operative spirituality, not the spirituality of Ignatius in his own day, that it is important for us to speak. We must compare it critically with present-day christologies, which do really set forth criteria of validity. No one can shield himself or herself with a past spirituality in order to ignore the course that christology has run since then and the problems that any serious interpretation of Christ must face up to today, no matter how 'spiritual' it may be.

Let us begin with the now well-known distinction between christologies 'from *above*' and christologies 'from *below*'. The word 'above' here alludes to the christological dogma that began to take shape in Jesus' own day and that eventually was enshrined in dogmatic formulas: e.g., that Jesus is the unique Son of God, consubstantial with the Father, one divine person in two complete natures, a human nature and a divine nature.

Long before the dogmatic formulas of Nicea and Chalcedon appear on the horizon, indeed in the New Testament itself, we find a notable example of this christology 'from *above*'. The prologue of the fourth Gospel describes the origin and divine essence of Jesus of Nazareth, and so it is able to inscribe his history within a divine plan.

With regard to a christology 'from *below*', i.e., one fashioned out of the very *history* of Jesus, we could say that we find no written example of such a christology in the New Testament. Even though they do not explicitly propound the divinity of Jesus of Nazareth, the Synoptics have already interpreted him, at the time of writing, as a prophet, the Messiah of Israel, and the Son of God, though not in such a precise sense as that meant in the fourth Gospel. None of them really starts off from below, from the history of Jesus uninterpreted by the witnesses (if that is possible).

What was the process whereby the evangelists or witnesses arrived at their interpretation, or interpretations, of Jesus? If we had some document that spelled out this hermeneutic process, that began with their uncertainty and indifference and ended with their adhesion and faith, then we would have precisely a christology 'from *below*', a christology from the human history of Jesus of Nazareth.

There is no doubt that the Gospels, especially the Synoptic Gospels, do provide us with data about this process. But neither is there any doubt that they frankly and explicitly present themselves, in general, as testimonies of faith that have *already* fashioned an interpretation of who Jesus of Nazareth was, despite appearances or through them. We must rescue the data about the 'historical' Jesus from this overall picture in which they are presented to us already interpreted.

We would have to make many specific points about these categories, and I shall make some of them at the proper time. But they will make more sense after I have applied this classification to the christology of the Ignatian Exercises.

There cannot be the slightest doubt that the christology of the Exercises is a christology from *above*. It could not be otherwise, if we consider the theology of Ignatius's day, and only some sort of inexplicable taboo could prompt people to say the contrary. The Second Week of the Exercises will confirm my opinion. It is possible that the vaunted claim that the christology of the Exercises is one from below derives from a misunderstanding of the Call of an Earthly King, which opens the Second Week and begins the various contemplations on the life of Christ.

When I talk about a 'misunderstanding', I am thinking of various factors that do not permit us to deduce a christology from that meditation, much less a christology from *below*. We must remember that the meditation on the earthly king is a sort of *parable*, as its very title indicates: The Call of an Earthly King 'will help us to contemplate the life of the eternal King' (91). As in every parable (that of the sower, for example), the logical attitude or approach in the secular or profane realm is translated to the religious realm and helps us to understand it. The problem for us here is that the force of Ignatius's argument in the first part of his parable is largely lost on us, and it does not dominate in the second part of the parable as it should.

We know so little about what a king is, what a personal call from a king to his subjects or 'knights' might mean, what the peculiar conditions he poses for the joint execution of an enterprise entail, that we lose nothing today by beginning with the second and presumably more well-known part: Christ the King and the following of him. And insofar as the second part becomes independent of the first part, we think we can find christological features in it.

If we retain the original sense of parable here, however, we find that the second part has to do more or less with the following question: What should we do logically if we encounter an 'eternal' King who operates as the earthly king does? Thus, within the mechanism of the meditation, the characteristics given to the eternal King are *hypothetical*. They do not derive from christology but from sociology or social psychology.

Some may object that this principle, though valid for studying any gospel parable, does not apply here, or does not apply so strictly. Why? Because Ignatius obviously has a very clear vision of the eternal King and hence almost distorts or unbalances his presentation of an earthly king and how he might operate.

I do not share that opinion, as a matter of fact. I think that we should not regard the figure of the eternal King as the product of any specific christology but rather as a psychological preparation for what Ignatius intends to present later. For the moment, however, let us accept the above opinion and see what sort of christology might be entailed.

Proponents of this opinion will say right away that Ignatius is talking about the historical following of Jesus, about an imitation of Christ that emphasizes what Jesus said and did in history: i.e., about a christology from *below*. So saying, these people have lost sight of the one who is making the call: not a craftsman from Nazareth as was the actual case in history, but the eternal King himself, God incarnate in Jesus. That accounts for the obligation to follow his call and, given the tremendous distance between God and the creature, the impulse to respond to such abasement by distinguishing oneself in the service of 'the eternal King and the Lord of all' and making 'offerings of greater value and of more importance'(97).

Before Jesus' first word or act, you see, comes the dogma of his divinity. He is the eternal King, and such an interpretation is christology from above: i.e., in terms of the attributes that theology and dogmatics attributed to Jesus of Nazareth after his life, death, and resurrection. Not any and every kind of interest in the *history* of Jesus betokens a christology from below. After all, the fourth Gospel is interested in the concrete words and deeds of Jesus of Nazareth, the incarnate Word of the Father. The writer of 1 John expresses the same 'historical' interest but begins as follows: "*what existed from the beginning*, what we have heard, what we have seen with our own eyes, what we have beheld and touched with our own hands . . . the word of life . . ." (1Jn 1:1).

The terms, *from below* and *from above*, allude to the starting point for reflection. In themselves they do not imply reductionism. A christology from above must take due account of the historical Jesus just as surely as a christology from below must ponder his relationship to God in its interpretation of the historical Jesus.

So we face two choices with respect to this meditation on the earthly king. Either it is a parable, and we must reserve christological qualifications for those meditations or contemplations that deal explicitly and specifically with Jesus. Or else we must view it as the starting point of a christology, in which case it is undoubtedly a christology from above, even if we are not told so.

Let us take the first hypothesis and look at the first contemplation of the Second Week, which narrates 'history' about Jesus. It is about nothing less than the Incarnation (101):" . . . how *the Three Divine Persons look down upon the whole expanse or circuit of all the earth*, filled with human beings. Since They see that all are going down to hell, *They decree in Their eternity that the Second Person should become man to save the human race . . .* " (102). It is hard to imagine how anyone could look at such a beginning and see anything but a christology from *above*: i.e., in terms of the place given to Jesus in the divine plan by theological interpretation (130). It is almost a more imaginative version of the Prologue of John's Gospel.

We have another datum in the same vein that is even more eloquent. Not only is Jesus' divinity associated with his glorification in the Resurrection (Rom 1:4), but it is not even related in any way to his message. It accompanies him forever and from the very start. Thus, the fifth contemplation of the Second Week "will consist in applying the five senses to the matter of the first and second contemplations" (121): i.e., to the contemplations on Jesus' Incarnation and Nativity. As we know, the 'application of senses' means applying the five senses, 'with the aid of the imagination', to that which has already been contemplated in a more rational manner or, to stick to Ignatius's terminology, employing 'the three powers' of memory, understanding, and will.

The application of the senses to the 'history', with the aid of the imagination, brings the contemplated event closer and makes it more vivid and compelling. Sight and hearing, the senses we use to know things and events in general terms, quite naturally present the object itself to our contemplation. The use of imaginative 'touch' fluctuates, since it does not always have a proper object of its own; its application may or may not help us to sense or understand the meaning of the object or get closer to its image. In the meditation on hell, for example, imaginative touch is used to bring us closer to the pain of the damned. Its proper object is the fire of hell. But since corporeal fire is not the essential thing in hell, Ignatius shifts our imagination to an *analogy*: "With the sense of touch to feel the flames which envelop and burn *the souls*" (70).

The difficulty already evident with the sense of touch becomes much more obvious with the senses of taste and smell. Their application also follows the routes of analogy and symbolism. In the same meditation on hell, the sense of taste is to get across to us "the bitterness of tears, sadness, and remorse of conscience" (69).

Now what about the application of senses in our contemplation of the Incarnation and the Nativity? Here we are "to smell *the infinite fragrance*, and taste *the infinite sweetness of the divinity*" (124).

Thus, awareness of the divinity that accompanies Jesus of Nazareth from his first to last steps on earth is an explicit and characteristic element in the Ignatian Exercises. So, for example, in the first contemplation of the Third Week (relating to the passion), the fifth point is "to consider how the divinity hides itself . . . " (196). And in the first contemplation of the Fourth Week (devoted to the Resurrection), the fourth point is "to consider the divinity, which seemed to hide itself during the passion, now appearing and manifesting itself . . . " (223).

Can anyone honestly doubt or deny that we are dealing with a christology from above? Granting that the answer is obvious, we are still confronted with several legitimate questions: What is so bad about that? Why, against all evidence and in an anachronistic way, try to free Ignatius of something that is supposedly a stigma?

II

We have a right to expect that any christology, no matter which end it starts from, will go in the other direction and end up at the opposite starting point. There is nothing to stop a christology that begins with the divinity of Jesus from exploring its own foundations and, by using present-day historical methods, ending up with the Jesus of history. Moreover, it is clear that Ignatius *believed* he had arrived at the Jesus of history. If he was mistaken, then, in principle, it was not because he began with the divinity of Jesus; it was because he did not possess the cognitive data that could have led him to the historical Jesus, such data not being proper to his time and place.

All that is true *in principle*. In actual fact, however, the risks are greater. If we begin with the divinity of Jesus, we need not necessarily distort the history of his life; but we run a great risk of doing precisely that, even with the best historical instruments at our disposal.

Speaking in general terms, I think the risks can be reduced to two. The first risk is that we will look at the history of Jesus from a certain angle that limits our vision. That angle is, precisely, our 'prior' conception of the 'divinity' attributed to Jesus from the very start. We have already noted how that happened to the biblical statement that 'God is love'. Although we know that Jesus is true human being, although we are aware of the *kenosis* or emptying of Jesus' divinity (Phil 2:7), it will always be difficult for us to rid ourselves of the notions dictated by our mind as to what divinity *must have been* in Jesus.

Examples of this are all the discussions about the simultaneity, or worse, interaction of the different modes of knowing, proper to God or to the human being, in the one person of Jesus. Extending the impeccability of God to Jesus of Nazareth, thanks to the dogma about his one person, we can see virtues where his contemporaries, more attuned to the historical context and relying on the ordinary criteria that apply to human actions, saw sins. Jesus was baptized as a sinner, and there was no element of 'theater' in that.

To fall into this temptation is all the more inevitable insofar as the evangelists themselves succumbed to its influence. I do not intend to stop here to prove the point. We need only recall what practically all exegetes recognize: the more human traits of Jesus that show up in the oldest Synoptic Gospel, that of Mark, perhaps because they were considered 'all too human', disappear from the other two Synoptic Gospels.

The second risk is closely linked to the first. The historical Jesus did not begin his ministry by letting his contemporaries know that he was God, or even the Messiah, and then offering proofs of that fact so that, once he had caught their interest, he could communicate a message about divine things that might or might not be of interest in themselves. On the contrary, the Jesus of history had to say something that was intrinsically interesting from the very beginning so that the historical repercussions of his message might attract attention to him.

Even though we may assume that he interested people as a wonderworker, his 'miracles' interested them only because they cured people, not because they were signs that Jesus possessed divinity. Indeed, moving from the status of wonderworker to teacher in the minds of his listeners constituted a real problem for Jesus. It led him to adopt a pedagogical approach that has come to be known, inadequately, as the 'messianic secret'.

Now if we assume from the very start that God could not possibly take an interest in human affairs, concrete human affairs in history, we will find it extraordinarily difficult to explain how Jesus of Nazareth began to arouse the interest and passion of his contemporaries, both for and against himself.

So let us assume we have a christology from above that succumbs to the two risks just discussed. What will be the result? Well, the most likely result would be the one epitomized in the title of one of the books that most influenced Ignatius and his Exercises: the *Imitation of Christ and Despising of the World*. Note that this is the only book explicitly suggested as reading material for the exercitant, aside from the Gospels and 'lives of the saints' in general (100). That is strictly and completely logical.

On the one hand, then, the risk is that of reducing Jesus' proposals, preferences, and attitudes to those judged compatible with the view that an absolute God would have to have of the whole relative world of creation. Jesus sees things as God sees them. Jesus-God is our model, then. In every event of his life there is some divine characteristic we are to grasp and make our own. His course is exemplary, subject neither to time nor the vicissitudes of any project. And his earthly journey leads to the cross because, without a doubt, the cross in itself is a value. The Resurrection is the model of what comes after the cross, in another life, the cross being the culmination of this life here.

On the other hand, Jesus does not attract human beings with any historical project. From the very beginning he is seen as trying to ensure that human beings do not go down into hell (102). To do that, in the name of the divinity dwelling in him, he proposes criteria that are wholly the opposite of those guiding human beings whose lives are oriented by a historical project. His passage from divinity to history does not give any divine cast to history, you see. On the contrary, it precludes the absolutization of history as well as the absolutization of the criteria guiding and governing it. Indeed, it introduces criteria that the world judges to be not only useless but foolish. To follow Christ is to shift our preferences, as he did, from every worldly, historical object to their eternal, divine object.

I think it would be hard to deny that this, in broad outline, is essentially the christology that dominates the last three weeks of the Ignatian Exercises.

Moreover, the christological vacuum prevailing in the First Week and at essential points of the Second Week, as we saw in the previous chapters, is intimately bound up with that christology. The fact is that a christology from *above* does not easily correct the idea of God with the history of Jesus, hence the christological vacuum; on the contrary, it depends essentially on that idea, if it does not overcome its attendant risks.

In the previous two chapters we saw that the revelation of Christ did not substantially alter the image of the divinity in its relationship to the creature. So of necessity, the christology we find explicitly in the Exercises dovetails with a theology that views human destiny as a test. Jesus contributes fundamental data to this test.

We must peruse the Exercises, especially the last three weeks, to see if my hypothesis is correct in its second part. In doing this, we must remember that Ignatius generally follows the gospel accounts and adds no comments in the contemplations of Jesus. So we may well find explicit data of his christology in the Notes that accompany the contemplations and, even more likely, in the parable-like meditations that Ignatius himself made up: e.g., the Call of an Earthly King, the Meditation on Two Standards, and the Three Kinds of Humility.

Let us begin with the Call of an Earthly King. Readers will recall that since it is a parable or comparison, it is doubtful we can deduce from it the *starting point* of Ignatius's christology in the Exercises: i.e., whether from above or below. Here, however, our focus is not its starting point but its *content and function*. Hence the comparison between the earthly king and the eternal King will provide us with several crucial elements of the christology of the Exercises.

Remember that in a parable the first term of the comparison is crucial. And the first thing that attracts our attention in Ignatius's parable is a certain disproportion between the vagueness surrounding the project of the king and the detailed nature of the proposal to follow him.

As far as the project is concerned, the king says: "It is my will to conquer all the lands of the infidel" (93). Given such a project, we would expect that the king would call different classes of people with different skills, aptitudes, and functions. But no, his call presents a criterion that is universal in its extent and very detailed in its comprehension: "whoever wishes to join with me in this enterprise must be content with the same food, drink, clothing, etc. *as mine*. So, too, he must work *with me* by day, and watch with me by night, etc., that *as* he has had a share in the toil with me, afterwards, he may share in the victory *with me*" (93).

It is quite obvious that the stress is much more on the behavior incumbent on the knight than on the objective necessities, value, and incidents of the enterprise. In other words: it is a call to the *imitation* of the king much more than, or in opposition to, a call to the creativity needed to achieve the desired result. The enterprise seems to be merely an opportunity or *occasion* for the knights to distinguish themselves in a service (97) that is defined in terms of emulation and imitation. Their service, in other words, comes down to the capacity to follow the one who is calling them, leading them, and giving them example, even in the most difficult and arduous ways.

The second part of the parable, which explains the above or applies it to Christ, the eternal King, merely confirms the christological elements we have drawn from the analogy. The enterprise is even vaguer: "It is my will to conquer the whole world and all my enemies" (95). Any possible trace of a historical enterprise is relativized by the eternal: "and thus to enter into the glory of my Father" (95). True enough, the imitation is not as detailed as in the first part of the comparison. It is reduced to this: "Therefore, whoever wishes to join me in this enterprise must be willing to labor with me, that by following me in suffering, he may follow me in glory" (95). But we should remember two things. First, it is the first description that sheds light on the second and fleshes out the notion of 'laboring with me'. Second, what is not made concrete here is made much more concrete further on. There is the offering of "those who wish to give greater proof of their love and to distinguish themselves" (97). Their following is more detailed and significant: "I protest that it is my earnest desire and my deliberate choice . . . to imitate Thee in bearing all wrongs and all abuse and all poverty, both actual and spiritual . . . " (98).

Quite obviously, the presupposed *divinity* of Christ, the eternal King, acts as a powerful stimulus to this imitation: I, God, did it, even though I am God. Will you not be capable of doing it, since it is so common in the human and temporal world?

Let us say, then, that the contemplations of Christ, which begin with the Call of an Earthly King, tend to make us desire "to know better the *eternal Word Incarnate* in order to *serve and follow* Him more closely" (130). But what we learn in them is not so much how to serve as how to follow, unless the first is merely a synonym of the second.

This fits in with an Ignatian element that has been adduced as proof that the christology of the Exercises is interested in the historical figure of Jesus, or even proof that it is a christology from below. I refer to the image of the 'unworthy slave'. In the contemplation of the Nativity, Ignatius wants us to *live* intensely what we are contemplating. This prompts him to suggest that we not simply be present passively in imagination and observe the unfolding story but try to enter the scene and become part of it: "I will make myself a poor little unworthy slave, and as though present, look upon them, contemplate them, and serve them in their needs with all possible homage and reverence" (114).[71]

Now if we look at this procedure, which logically is used in the remaining contemplations of the life of Jesus, we see that the intention is clear: to know better in order to imitate better. The word 'serve', at least here, is itself employed as a factor in this knowing that is geared to imitation.

Let us say, then, that we have come to know the king but little about his enterprise. Perhaps we can come to understand his enterprise better through his 'standard', since this word is often used metaphorically to designate the *project* a person wants to see through. Here again, however, we are surprised to discover that imitation does not really let us penetrate or get inside the plan or project of the eternal King, who is now called 'the sovereign and true Commander'. (Perhaps we are no longer so surprised, after all, since we are beginning to catch on to the logic of this christology.) We learn the concrete purpose of this meditation from what Ignatius has us ask for: " . . . for a knowledge of the *true life* exemplified in the sovereign and true Commander, and the grace to *imitate Him*" (139).

It is worth noting and pointing out the shift from eternal King to sovereign Commander, and from sovereign Commander to someone we might well describe better, in line with the content of the meditation, as a preacher of wisdom. Note what is said in the third point of the second part of the meditation: "Consider the address [*el sermón*] which Christ our Lord makes to all . . . recommending to them to seek to help all, first by attracting them to the highest spiritual poverty, and . . . even to actual poverty. Secondly, they should lead them to a desire for insults and contempt, for from these springs humility. . . . From these three steps, let them lead men to all other virtues" (146). In the colloquy we ask for all these things from Christ our Lord, 'thereby to imitate him better' (147).

At this point it is important, I think, that we go back and see, from what we have just read, the exact nature of the enterprise the eternal King had in mind for us to share when he said that his will was 'to conquer the whole world and all my enemies' (95). Here we have the enemies fleshed out in the vices that figure in the Standard of Satan. The demons are to lay snares for human beings and bind them with chains, leading them to covet riches, the empty honors of this world, overweening pride, and then all the other vices (142). Thus, the world conquered by Christ is the soul of the human being, now freed from the 'snares and chains' of the Devil and led to all the virtues. That would be the eternal King's conquest of all his enemies.

Here we discover the divine function that Ignatius sees in the Incarnation, in the sojourn of the Second Person of the Trinity on earth. Besides giving us the laws that definitively establish what is commanded and what is prohibited, he gives us the *divine example* of how to live. He tells us what God values in the attitudes and behavior patterns of human beings by mirroring them as God-made-human.

It is by contemplating God Incarnate that our 'indifference', within the realm of the licit, is to find a profounder criterion for our humility: i.e., the *preferences of Jesus*. Writes Ignatius: "The third kind of humility . . . is the most perfect kind of humility. It consists in this. If we suppose the first and second kind attained, then whenever the praise and glory of the Divine Majesty would be equally served, *in order to imitate and be in reality more like* Christ our Lord, I desire and choose poverty with Christ poor, rather than riches; insults with Christ loaded with them, rather than honors; I desire to be accounted as worthless and a fool for Christ, rather than to be esteemed as wise and prudent in this world. So Christ was treated before me" (167).

From a christological standpoint it is highly instructive that Jesus is coming to be turned into a more concrete criterion than the law, but that this concreteness is not accompanied by any *purpose*: i.e. by any element pointing to a historical project that demanded these attitudes of Jesus or was the reason why he had to adopt them. We see *the cross* taking on increasing value and importance as such, far beyond any that might be derived from an attentive reading of the Gospels, even in Ignatius's time.

In the second contemplation of the Nativity in the Second Week, we read: "This will be to see and consider what they are doing, for example, making the journey and laboring *that* [*para que*] our Lord *might* be born in extreme poverty, and *that* [*para*] after many labors, after hunger, thirst, and cold, after insults and outrages, He *might* die on the cross, and all this for me" (116).

Here we can perceive the risks of a christology from above. Divinity, the notion of which accompanies and guides the reading of events, focuses on the most central events, the passion in this case, and disregards the others as merely accidental or instrumental.

Even if we assume the strict historicity of the infancy narratives, for example, the assumption that Mary and Joseph journeyed and labored *so that* (*para que*) Jesus might be born in extreme poverty runs counter to the direct testimony of Luke, which tells us that Joseph and Mary went to the inn and did not want Jesus to be laid in a manger when he was born. Here the divinity-passion relationship is superimposed on the reading of history. Ignatius also loses sight of the fact that nowhere in the Gospels does Jesus appear to go out looking for poverty, abuses, or death. He accepts them because his mission confronts him with the alternative of enduring them or giving up that mission. Also lost sight of is the fact that the historical Jesus was unable to interest his contemporaries insofar as he was disposed to endure extreme poverty, all kinds of insults and affronts, and the cross. History, even as Ignatius could read it in the Gospels in his own day, shows us that his disciples, those most interested in him, believed *despite that*.

The reading from above also alters the proportion of events. Up to the moment of his passion Jesus undoubtedly had a difficult life, but not particularly difficult if we consider the vast majority of his contemporaries. He was aided economically in his ministry. Far from receiving continual affronts and insults, he frequently got admiration, thanks, and such devoted adhesion that it alarmed the authorities and prompted them to assassinate him. Why didn't Ignatius read all this? Because events are 'projected' to the final image of God crucified on a cross. There is no interest as to why the historical Jesus ended up on a cross. Since he is God, those who bring him to the cross are mere instruments. God must have a divine reason for dying on a cross, and that is what matters.

Thus, the third kind of humility and the christology of the Exercises in general take the cross as an *end*. As such, it can appear only as the end of a moral lesson. Otherwise, it would have to be taken as a means: clearly unwanted but accepted out of fidelity to the historical project in which such a death was inscribed as necessary.

When it is set up as an end, then the cross shows up as the exemplary victory over 'all the enemies'. For the latter are no longer real, historical persons but the eternal enemies of humanity before God: the Devil (142), the world (97,167), and the flesh (95,157).

Similarly, in the Three Classes of Men and the Three Kinds of Humility, the virtues of Jesus are wholly centered around the unique event of the passion; that is his 'doctrine' (145). This 'doctrine' of his is summed up by J. Roothaan, a great expert on the Exercises, in the following words in his spiritual diary: "Everything agreeable is to be rejected by the mere fact that it is agreeable. Everything disagreeable is to be sought by the very fact that it is disagreeable, unless some just motive persuades us of the contrary—or better, unless some just and certain motive of service and divine glory commands the contrary of us."[72]

This logical and authorized version of the third kind of humility, and of the essentials of the christology of the Exercises, is not simply the result or effect of a masochistic outlook. Logically at least, it is the consistent continuation of the test-theology, the essential presence of which in the Exercises I sought to verify in the preceding chapters. The test itself *does not require* anything more than the fulfillment of the law (95,165). But since it is such a dangerous matter and the human being is so inclined to evil, Jesus comes to 'help out' (146). He does this by showing, in his life and especially in his passion, how we are to orient our preferences to make this fulfillment of the law not only possible but probable. He thus helps us to overcome the 'snares' and 'chains' (142) wherewith the enemies of humanity take advantage of our preferences, put them in disorder, and thus lead us to the breaking of the law, i.e., to the 'vices' opposed to the commandments of God.

Resurrection is the living testimony of victory at the judgment. It is what follows after having 'followed me in my labors' (93,95). Union with the resurrected Christ is not conceived as an element of the redemptive project, as Paul conceives it in Romans 4:25; it is what follows the divine judgment. Union with this victorious Christ, then, is an important element of the *preference* that leads imitation toward the Christ of the cross.

In this way christology converts *indifference* into *preference*. The anthropology of the Exercises, then, is adapted to the concrete and unbalanced conditions in which the test of the human being takes place.[73] And it is not strange that christology should have this function, as I have already pointed out. Since it is a christology from *above*, the prior idea of divinity and what suits it powerfully influences the reading of the Gospels and the contemplations based on them.

But we must not forget that the preference under consideration here, however much affected it may be by christology, is nevertheless subordinated to a higher criterion. I left out this criterion in the texts cited in this chapter. It can be summed up in the formulation of the Call of an Earthly King: " . . . provided only it is for Thy greater service and praise" (98; see 147,155,167,179–81).

This higher criterion will occupy us in the following chapter.

CHAPTER V

Demythologization and Discernment of Spirits

I

The use of *mythical* language to refer to the interventions of God in history is not a specifically christological problem, but it has been posed especially with reference to the revelation and activity of God in Jesus Christ. That fact may be somewhat accidental; but there is no doubt that no christology from *above*, in which the idea of divinity is present from the very start, can evade the issue. We have already seen that such is the case with the Ignatian Exercises.

Summarizing the problematic of Rudolf Bultmann, we can say that we have *myth* or *mythical language* whenever: (a) an internal or subjective experience of an encounter with the Absolute is located outside as an event that has taken place in the objective realm; (b) one talks about a supernatural causality operating like, and among, the other natural causes of phenomena; (c) a twofold history is thereby produced—a profane history in which only the latter natural causes are operative, and a 'sacred' history which takes into account and narrates the interruptions of profane history provoked by interventions due to supernatural causality.

Miracles narrated as such, and hence events such as the Incarnation and Resurrection of course, fit completely into the above three categories of *the mythical*. Now in this regard, the Ignatian Exercises unsuspiciously and faithfully follow the gospel narratives, so we can readily conclude that the problems and inconveniences of mythical language apply to the Exercises as well—although, as I noted in Volume II (Appendix I), the gospel narratives of the Resurrection are far more sober vis-à-vis the mythical than many other religious documents.

What are the problems and inconveniences? The most obvious one is often brought up, and it is of an apologetic nature: modern human beings, educated in a scientific mentality and idiom, cannot accept such 'myths'; they are

76

impervious to them. Modern people read the Gospels as we Christians read the
Iliad. In short, modern human beings cannot picture a God who intervenes in
the world that way.

In fact, theological reasons of a more central nature could well be added
here. These kinds of interventions, soundly or unsoundly labelled 'mythical',
presuppose that God acts now and again to alter the course and influence of
natural and human causes because God deems it advisable. But it may well
be that we have not pondered some of the consequences of such a presupposi-
tion.

One consequence of no little importance is that this makes God responsible,
by action or omission, for everything that happens in the world, with all the
implied dose of inhumanity. Another consequence is that one can hardly see the
necessity, suggested by Jesus, of praying to God that his will be done 'on earth
as it is in heaven'. If it is true that God does not have any limitation on the
exercise of his will through direct interventions of his power and that he has not
imposed any limitation on this use, then he could just as well intervene all the
time as well as now and then.

Needless to say, I cannot analyze here the arguments of Bultmann, the
theologian whose name is most closely associated with the solution known as
'demythologization'. Although various other theologians went much further
than he did, he was the first to present the problem in a clear and systematic
way.

I would point out, however, that the term 'demythologization' is misleading.
Bultmann does not suggest that we simply rid ourselves of any and every
'mythical' narrative. He says that we must interpret them. We do that by once
again putting back in our inner 'existential' world what the myth projected into
the outer world of objects and objective events. Thus the *fact*, if not the event,
retains its crucial and even theological value.

Insofar as that is concerned, one could possibly say that the Ignatian
Exercises seem to pass the test of demythologization fairly well, at least with
respect to Christ. Perhaps that would properly apply to any spirituality as
opposed to theological christologies, since the latter are obliged to explain what
they mean exactly by such divine interventions in history. By contrast, a
spirituality characteristically tends to interpret 'sacred' events in existential
terms all the time, whatever its proponents might think about their occurrence
or nonoccurrence in the outside world.

Thus, there is no doubt that Ignatius, like all Christians of his day, accepted
the external reality of the divine interventions in the Old and New Testaments.
But we can certainly say that Ignatius always interprets Jesus existentially in the
Exercises. What really interests him finds expression in the purpose of each
contemplation: "Then I will *reflect on myself* that I may *reap some fruit*" (114
and *passim*).

But will that 'reflection on myself' in the light of the contemplated events be
the existential reflection that Bultmann has in mind? The demythologization
proposed by Bultmann, you see, does not consist in any sort of reflection

whatsoever that one might undertake regarding one's own life vis-à-vis some supposed divine intervention in the objective world.

Bultmann rightly insists that there is a *hermeneutic circle* in my way of approaching the deeds of God and interpreting them. If all of them are not to be associated with external events but rather with what God is saying to me and my life, then obviously my possibilities of hearing and understanding the divine message, of 'reaping some fruit' by 'reflecting on myself', will be proportionate to what could be called my level of existential understanding. The circle of interpretation (i.e., the hermeneutic circle) means that a better or higher level of reflection on my existence and the factors conditioning it will enable me to grasp things in the word of God that a more superficial and inauthentic way of life would not notice. Those who better hear the word of God and its demands, in turn, get down deeper into that existential level; and thus they become better prepared to hear more profoundly what God is saying to them. So goes the circle on and on.

Moreover, Bultmann proposes a concrete procedure or methodology for *authenticating* our existential reflection and thus preparing ourselves to better hear and more profoundly understand the word that God is addressing to us when we interpret supposedly mythical events. That procedure is, of course, Heidegger's analysis of the differences between an authentic existence and an inauthentic existence, which is to be found in his well-known work, *Being and Time.*

Here I shall not consider whether Bultmann did or did not understand Heidegger correctly. That is an issue which I discussed a bit in Volume II, Chapter III (pp. 31–39) of this series. In any case, Heidegger had an ontological intention that Bultmann rejected. Bultmann felt we should not look to Heidegger for the results of an abstract (*existenzial*) phenomenology of human existence, but rather should look to him for a concrete 'existentialist' (*existenziell*) analysis. If we approach *Being and Time* this later way, we will find a methodological analysis that will help us very much to deepen and perfect our own level of existential understanding. In a sense, then, we will find in Heidegger a sort of spiritual pathway or course of 'exercises' that will help us to reach or get closer to an authentic existence and, says Bultmann, to understand as well as we can what God is trying to say to us through the events in Christ's life.

Now if we disregard the differences in chronology and themes, we cannot help but be struck by the similarity or parallelism with the criteria that Ignatius offers in his Exercises for approaching the contemplation of Christ. First of all, right from the start the Exercises explicitly mention the aim of authenticity: "Spiritual Exercises, which have as their purpose the conquest of self and the *regulation of one's life* in such a way that no decision is made *under the influence of any inordinate attachment*" (21).

In the Introductory Observations, Ignatius also talks about those who can and cannot go through the whole course of Exercises. If we look for the key to the basic requirement, we could well say that the crucial factor has a lot to do with the *truth* that the exercitant possesses, or should possess, in order to confront the *truth* he will encounter in the Exercises. In short, what is at stake is the hermeneutic circle.

This capacity for truth has something to do with intellectual capacity (18), but a lot more to do with the convergence and consistency of the whole human being: what we today might also call 'authenticity'.

We need only recall a few of these conditions. The exercitant should be 'disengaged', i.e., capable of concentrating on the essential: "In this seclusion the mind is not engaged in many things, but can give its whole attention to *one single interest . . .* " (20). The exercitant should also approach this encounter with the interior truth of 'magnanimity and generosity toward his Creator and Lord', offering God 'his entire will and liberty' (5). It is further assumed that this will and liberty are real, not imaginary, and capable of transforming things. Hence the complete Exercises are not to be given to people 'with little natural ability or of little physical strength' who would derive little or no profit from them (18).

When we move from these general preconditions, which are certainly quite demanding, to more detailed stipulations, we get an even clearer picture of the exercitant that Ignatius has in mind. He is a person capable of thinking, judging, and acting with all the powers of his being converging on a single point: his encounter with the truth wherein his destiny is to be decided.

The exercitant should be alone. Progress in the Exercises will be greater, "the more the exercitant withdraws from all friends and acquaintances, and from all worldly cares" (20). In this crucial encounter he should also keep his director "faithfully informed about the various disturbances and thoughts caused by the action of different spirits" (17). He should also avoid all curiosity, not only about worldly matters but also about the various stages of the process he is going through: "While the exercitant is engaged in the First Week of the Exercises, it will be helpful if he knows nothing of what is to be done in the Second Week. Rather, let him labor to attain what he is seeking in the First Week as if he hoped to find no good in the Second" (11,127).

Authenticity should fill him completely and pervade the whole process, as we learn from the Additional Directions. First of all, it should fill every moment of his time: "After retiring, just before falling asleep, for the space of a *Hail Mary*, I will think of the hour when I have to rise, and *why* I am rising, and briefly sum up the exercise I have to go through" (73); "When I wake up, *I will not permit my thoughts to roam at random*, but will turn my mind at once to the subject I am about to contemplate" (74). During the day the exercitant must have thoughts that are consonant with the feelings that should logically be evoked by a given contemplation (78), adapting everything to this end: i.e., lighting (79), bodily posture (76), eating (83,130), and the whole surrounding material context (130).

In short, it is a whole human existence that is going out to meet a word or message, and preparing itself to understand it, explore it, feel it, assimilate it, and carry it out as much as possible.

In this section dealing with the existential preparation for authenticity, I deliberately omitted any reference to discerning and knowing the import of the various movements or experiences—sad or happy, agitated or peaceful—that are felt by the spirit. That will be the subject of the next section.

II

Having reached this point, we must now bring together and briefly summarize certain elements that can no longer be examined in isolation.

From the preceding chapters there gradually surfaced the unknown quantum of an ultimate criterion for choosing a way of life, a criterion above and beyond the christological criterion (i.e., the imitation of Jesus). The first criterion that demolished indifference was the law, first in grave matter (the first kind of humility) and then in venial matter (the second kind of humility). After this 'christological vacuum', as I called it, came a second criterion, which was indeed linked to Jesus and to a christology from above centered around imitating Jesus, and particularly his sufferings (the third kind of humility).

Unexpectedly, however, indifference reappeared somehow because one could not take for granted that this real, concrete imitation of Jesus was indeed the *greater service* to the Divine Majesty. So what might be the third and ultimate criterion? Or, more to the point, how is one to find it and put it into practice in choosing?

We just saw in the previous section the enormous importance that Ignatius attaches to a totally integrated human being, affective and effective disposability, and existential authenticity. It is noteworthy that Ignatius tells directors not to go beyond the First Week with exercitants who do not meet those requirements or preconditions. The latter preconditions could be called *hermeneutic* or interpretive ones, for it really is a matter of interpreting the word that is going to be addressed to the exercitant as ultimate criterion. This can be summed up in a note from the hand of Ignatius himself that is similar to what we find in the Exercises (18): "If some do not seem to have the dispositions of spirit such that much fruit might be expected of them, it will suffice to give them the Exercises of the *First Week* and stop there, until their thirst for more suggests that more profit is to be expected of them."[74]

We might well ask: Why the limitation? What is there about the material after the First Week that makes the Exercises unsuitable for the kind of people that Ignatius rejects? Two hypotheses suggest themselves. One is that it has something to do with the christological element of the Exercises; the other is that it has to do with the mysterious ultimate criterion for choosing a way of life.

My own view, of course, is that it is the second possibility that underlies the issue. Ignatius certainly did not think that contemplations on the life and sufferings of Christ could be superfluous for, or harmful to, anyone. The point is, you see, that in the mind of Ignatius the Exercises were not solely or mainly a way of knowing Christ and imitating him. The contemplations on Christ and the resultant intent to imitate him are framed in, and oriented to, a 'way of making a choice of a way of life'. That is why Ignatius tells the director not to go beyond the First Week with some people and specifically writes: "But let him not go on further and *take up the matter dealing with the Choice of a Way of Life . . .* " (18).

At this point we can surmise that the discovery or discernment of this *third criterion* for choosing a way of life, which tops the christological criterion, is very delicate and demands the fullest possible authenticity from the exercitant.

So I now combine the two hypotheses we have been studying into one: knowing whether God does or does not want me for the strictest imitation of Jesus and a greater service to his Divine Majesty is going to depend on my hearing his voice, his call, in and through my inner experiences *while* I am reflecting on the matter of the Exercises.

In this connection it is worth noting that the first thing Ignatius hits on when the *matter* of the Exercises does not arouse such inner movements is to check out the criteria of *authenticity* that I mentioned in the previous section: "When the one who is giving the Exercises perceives that the exercitant is not affected by any spiritual experiences, such as consolations or desolations, and that he is not troubled by different spirits, *he ought to ply him with questions* about the exercises. He should ask him whether he makes them at the appointed times, and how he makes them. He should question him about the Additional Directions, whether he is diligent in the observance of them. He will demand an account in detail of each one of these points" (6).[75]

Here we really come face to face with an essential point of the theology of the Exercises: Ignatius's absolute confidence that when the exercitant invests his whole life in following the unfolding of the two previous criteria day after day and week after week, the word of God will make itself heard, providing the elements of the third criterion, the greater service and praise of his Divine Majesty.

This shows up even more explicitly when Ignatius urges the director not to manipulate the *matter* of the Exercises. For only thus can one be sure that it will be God who will use the interior experiences of the exercitant to reveal the final criterion, a criterion that is personal for the individual exercitant rather than general like the previous ones. This first comes out when Ignatius writes: "The one who explains to another the method and order of meditating or contemplating should narrate accurately the facts of the contemplation or meditation. Let him adhere to the points, and add only a short or summary explanation. The reason for this is that when one in meditating takes the solid foundation of facts, and goes over it and reflects on it for himself, he may find something that makes them a little clearer or better understood. This may arise *either from his own reasoning, or from the grace of God enlightening his mind.* Now this produces greater spiritual relish and fruit than if one in giving the Exercises had explained and developed the meaning at great length" (2).

But this observation for the director becomes crucial when it has to do with not manipulating the will of the exercitant, for only there is the second criterion given in the Introductory Observations (2) above to be taken as the final criterion: "The director of the Exercises ought not to urge the exercitant more to poverty or any promise than to the contrary, nor to one state of life or way of living more than to another. . . . While one is engaged in the Spiritual Exercises, it is more suitable and much better *that the Creator and Lord in person communicate Himself to the devout soul* in quest of the divine will. . . . Therefore, the director of the Exercises . . . *should permit the Creator to deal directly with the creature, and the creature directly with his Creator and Lord*" (15).

Let us focus for a moment on this essential point of the theology of the Ignatian Exercises, on which the final criterion of choosing a way of life is going to depend. Indeed, let us pose the problem clearly and straightforwardly. The language used by Ignatius here is obviously 'mythical' in the sense we have defined above.

It very often happens that in the spiritual heat of the Exercises themselves people do not pay much attention to the exact character of the language Ignatius uses with reference to God. Everything is spiritual and divine in a certain sense, and language consistent with this atmosphere seems natural and appropriate. Something of the same sort also occurs when people discuss the Exercises. Moreover, the original formulas of Ignatius, in Spanish at least, have a fresh and unexpected tang that makes us forget their literal content to some extent.

The fact is, you see, that the literal content of Ignatius's remarks here, and in other places we shall examine further on, pose a serious theological problem that is very definitely related to christology.

Do we literally think or believe that a given consolation or desolation is a *direct, personal* communication from God or Satan to the exercitant, just as some people think that the severity or duration of a flood is due to divine intervention or God's specific will? Or would we attribute the consolation or desolation to psychological causes, just as we attribute a flood to meteorological causes?

Before we can discuss the issue, we must clarify several elements in our formulation of the matter.

First of all, although it is certainly true that Ignatius was a keen observer of psychological laws for his time and place, there can be no doubt that he would answer the first question posed above with a resounding 'yes'. His statements cited above are clear and eloquent, and his Rules for the Discernment of Spirits (313–36) are couched in the same unequivocal language. It is not just a matter of expression or language, however. Numerous elements of an even more central nature point in the same direction, as we shall see in the course of this discussion.

Here I cannot dwell on all of them since not all of them relate to my purpose, which is not theological but rather historical and concerned with our present. One of them is relevant here, however: the third criterion could not be the crucial and final one if it were not *sure and certain*. In setting it above all other criteria, Ignatius almost always phrases it as the greater service of God. We may logically assume, then, that God makes clear what this service is, and that God does so to *each one* of the individuals who ask God about it from the general stance of authenticity required by the Exercises. For the *general* criterion of the imitation of Christ eventually becomes an *individual* problem: Where do God and God's service call me in this imitation?

Here we cannot help but be a bit anachronistic. If we assume that the signs given by interior movements do not come 'immediately' from God or the Devil, that they must be mediated and interpreted by means of the various currents of depth psychology that are in competition today, we may also assume that Ignatius would reject that sort of *reductionist* view of his criterion as totally alien to his intent and his faith.

My second point, by way of clarification, is closely associated with the first. Those who lean to the second alternative suggested in my questions about the causes of consolation or desolation and who feel that psychological causes are involved here need not thereby give up the idea of interpreting consolations and desolations as a criterion, even a criterion coming from God. Even when *demythologized*, the criterion continues to exist. But since the criterion is no longer regarded as a *direct* manifestation of God's will for a human being, and since psychology has moved from the realm of mere intuition where it was in Ignatius's time to the realm of the human sciences, the criterion associated with inner movements and experiences must also be interpreted by those same sciences.

But the main problem for this second position is not so much that the sign is no longer a 'sign from heaven' but a 'sign of the times', to use the idiom of the Gospels, and hence not *sure*. The problem does not lie so much in the manifest incapacity of the human sciences to provide categorical answers but in the impossibility of relating its criteria to the 'greater service and praise of God our Lord'.

These two clarifications lead us to a tentative but very important conclusion: We mus. be honest with ourselves and the exercitants on this matter. We are using a 'mythical' language that suits the overall atmosphere of the Exercises. Caught up in the enthusiasm evoked by what they discover in this powerful process of introversion, which they may be undertaking for the first time in their lives, the exercitants may well forget the peculiar nature of the language being addressed to them. Later on, back in secular life once again, they may wake up to find themselves asking questions about the coherence of the criteria used in the Exercises with the criteria they use in the other areas of life.

Here I certainly cannot discuss the overall issue of demythologization. But I will consider the theological problem posed to us by this direct communication of the Creator with the creature in the experiencing of such inner movements as consolation and desolation.

I have already brought up some of the inconveniences associated with attributing intentional causality to God in the occurrence of human events. Today theology is certainly reluctant to recognize any such interventions— which would not differ substantially from what we call 'miracles'—unless very weighty arguments compel theology to draw that conclusion. Let us see if such weighty arguments exist here in our case.

My investigation amounts to offering proof for a very tempting hypothesis regarding Ignatius. I have already said that he took for granted the Creator's immediate communications with the creature, at least *within the Exercises*. We could hardly have expected anything different in his age. In his age all mystical communication—the century of Ignatius was a century of mystics—was regarded as an immediate divine intervention as surely as the miracles of Christ were so regarded, only in this case the miracle took place inside the person.

It seems quite clear that Ignatius thought it was possible to view as mystical the inner experiences that took place in the spirit of the exercitant, under the conditions indicated above. A typical sign of this view is an observation which I left out in the passage cited above. The observation is this: *"Outside the Exercises*, it is true, we may lawfully and meritoriously urge [*mover*] all . . . to choose continence, virginity, the religious life, and every form of religious perfection [*perfección evangélica*]. But while one is engaged *in the Spiritual Exercises*, it is more suitable and much better that *the Creator and Lord in person* communicate Himself to the devout soul. . . . Therefore, the director of the Exercises . . . *should permit the Creator to deal directly with the creature, and the creature directly with his Creator and Lord"* (15). This distinction between 'urging' or 'moving' people outside or inside the Exercises is clear enough: while natural causes and their corresponding criteria are operative outside the Exercises, in the Exercises there are supernatural causes at work that must be respected as a higher criterion no longer in the hands of the director.

To be sure, the allusion to mystical phenomena hardly eliminates the problem of 'demythologizing' the language used—far from it! Yet, to my knowledge, very few theologians who specialize in spirituality have taken the trouble to explore the issue.[76]

One of the merits of Ignatius, in fact, though he did not tackle this problem since it postdated his own time, is his usual cautiousness outside the Introductory Observation I have just cited (15). Ignatius is usually very wary about assuming that the interior movements or experiences of the exercitant are immediate communications from God. This datum is of the utmost importance.

In the Exercises we find that there are three 'times' for making a choice of a way of life. I have already commented on the third time in discussing the criteria we have examined so far. It is what Ignatius describes as a 'time of tranquillity' (177f.).

It does not seem that either of the two ways of choosing a way of life in this third time could be called an 'immediate communication' of the Creator to the creature. An additional reason for thinking this is that, in 'weighing' or 'reckoning' (*raciocinando*) by the rules given in the Exercises for this time, we find that the ultimate criterion for choosing, beyond moving toward a greater likeness to Christ, still seems vague and indefinite (181). We find proof in this statement: "After such a choice or decision, the one who has made it must turn with great diligence to prayer in the presence of God our Lord, and offer Him his choice *that the Divine Majesty may deign* to accept and *confirm* it if it is for His greater service and praise" (183; see 188).

It seems that Ignatius is not content to let the choice end with the simple 'weighing' or 'reckoning' of the exercitant. He still looks for the immediate communication of the Creator to the creature as the ultimate criterion. If that has not occurred in the tranquil time of weighing, he expects that afterwards, in prayer, that communication will take place in the form of confirmation, i.e., in the form of spiritual movements that certify divine origin and the decisive criterion for choosing.

By contrast with that third time of tranquillity, the first time is what we might call the time of a 'miraculous call' or vocation: "When God our Lord so moves and attracts the will that a devout soul without hesitation, or the possibility of hesitation, follows what has been manifested to it. *St. Paul and St. Matthew acted thus* in following Christ our Lord" (175).

With this 'first time' it seems that Ignatius is trying to respect God's freedom, to call a person miraculously as and when God chooses, rather than pointing to any probable or logical outcome of the process involved in the Exercises. The examples themselves suggest the extraordinary occurrence, the unprepared 'miracle', to which all the criteria sought in the course of the Exercises must bow their head. I would be very much inclined to say that Ignatius's whole style and life reveal a decided inclination toward 'prepared' or 'assisted' miracles.

Two additional observations of Ignatius strongly suggest that he is not much inclined to acknowledge this mode of choice unless there is no doubt about the fact and the irresistible, supernatural nature of its force. In the Introductory Observations he writes: "If the one who is giving the Exercises sees that the exercitant is going on in consolation and in great fervor, he must admonish him not to be inconsiderate or hasty in making any promise or vow" (14). In short, the exercitant is not to make a choice on the assumption or belief that he is in the first time of choice.

Ignatius's second observation has a more profound theological sense. As Ignatius sees it, there is practically *only one* sure criterion, in itself not requiring the scrutiny of the director, that the Creator is communicating truly and immediately with the creature: "God alone can give consolation to the soul *without any previous cause*. It *belongs solely* to the Creator to come into a soul, to leave it, to act upon it. . . . I said *without previous cause*, that is, *without any preceding perception or knowledge of any subject by which a soul might be led to such a consolation through its own acts of intellect and will*" (330).

Here I shall not discuss the obviously 'mythical' content of this supposition, or its chances of convincing depth psychology that such a thing takes place 'without any previous cause'. The interesting thing I want to point up here is this. Ignatius tells us that "when consolation is without previous cause, as was said, there can be no deception in it, since it can proceed from God our Lord only" (336). Now this might easily be confused or equated with the 'first time' of choice, but it really should not and cannot be if we look at the matter closely.

It is clear that 'choosing' means having the possible option before one's mind (one's intellect and will); so any consolation deriving from that would be, by Ignatius's definition, *with cause*, hence not decisive. Furthermore, Ignatius is careful to warn about a possible error. *After* a *consolation without previous cause* and hence certainly divine, the exercitant may look at the choice in question and take the *prior* consolation without cause as the criterion for determining which path he should take, without considering the fact that the source of the sure criterion has already passed. Hence the exercitant "who has received such a consolation must consider it very attentively, and must cautiously distinguish the *actual time* of the consolation from the period which *follows* it. At such a time the soul is still fervent and favored with the grace and *aftereffects* of the consolation which *has passed*" (336). Since this fervor is no longer a sure sign of the will of God communicated immediately, neither can it be a sure sign of a choice in the 'first time'. In this case 'concepts and judgments' have already intervened: "In this second period the soul frequently forms various resolutions and plans which are not granted *directly* by God our Lord. They may come from our own reasoning on the relations of our concepts and on the consequences of our judgments, or they may come from the good or evil spirit. Hence, they must be *carefully examined* before they are given full approval and put into execution" (336).

Thus, Ignatius makes clear that it would be dangerous to confuse or equate the 'first time' of choice with seemingly similar situations that might arise in the course of the Exercises. Everything suggests that he views the 'first time' as something rare and extraordinary, something not related to the spiritual strategy that the Exercises proffer and implement.

So we are left with the 'second time' as the one undoubtedly preferred by Ignatius and considered by him as the result of the spiritual method he proposes. For the other two times, as we have just seen, do not have any *intrinsic* relationship with his Exercises.[77]

Ignatius describes the 'second time' as follows: "When much light and understanding are derived through *experience* of desolations and consolations and *discernment of diverse spirits*" (176).

The first relevant observation is that the key word, *experience*, denotes both a *certain amount of experimentation* and learning how to *discern*—i.e., to direct oneself—in and through that process of experimentation.

With respect to the first item, Ignatius does spell out how to go about preparing for one's choice during the Second Week; interestingly enough, however, he does not set a precise period of time for making it. It is as if he said: *don't* make your choice *before* preparing yourself with the Three Classes of Men and the Three Kinds of Humility. He places the rules for making one's choice, without any concrete indication of time, at the end of the Second Week; thus, the exercise that follows these rules is the first of the Third Week. After indicating that there are three times for making a good choice, he discusses the two ways to make a choice in the third time of tranquillity; only the first of these two ways seems like a meditation, containing six points but no preambles or preparatory prayer such as we usually find when Ignatius is offering a carefully arranged and temporally specified exercise. I think the conclusion we can draw from this fact is that the exercitant's process of choosing can cover a fairly unlimited period of experimentation in the Exercises: i.e., from the consideration of the Three Kinds of Humility to the end of the Third Week.[78]

Having entered the Exercises with magnanimity to make some sort of decision about his way of life and destiny, the exercitant learns how to discern or differentiate the movements in his soul with the help of the director before the start of the Third Week. After he has meditated on the Three Kinds of Humility, it is assumed that this experience, assisted by the director, can be applied to discovering the final criterion for deciding where God wants him for God's service. And it is precisely there that Ignatius assumes that the interior movements, properly interpreted, are to be understood as an immediate communication of the Creator to the creature regarding what the Creator wants concretely and personally from the creature. The Rules for the Discernment of Spirits at the end of the Exercises are "for understanding to some extent the different movements produced in the soul" (313).

III

A detailed commentary on those rules lies outside my christological purposes. I would remind my readers that the central problem of this chapter is to explain the relationship between the final criterion of choosing a way of life on the one hand and the 'mythical' language used to talk about an immediate, concrete, personal communication of God, along with interior movements, in order to establish that final criterion and enable the exercitant to choose in conformity with it.

The more we progress in our analysis, however, the less we can see any role for this supposed immediate communication from God. Indeed, whenever we talk about it, we almost have to force our language in order to avoid talking about an *immediate* communication *mediated* (!) through consolations and desolations.

It is these *mediations*, in fact, that are going to give us the criterion; but they never give it as proceeding from God. Instead, they give it through a process of prudent interpretation that is basically codified by Ignatius, adopted by the director, and then turned into an experience of *discernment* in the exercitant.

The almost miraculous intervention of God to establish the ultimate criterion disappears; at least we cannot see its necessity or its function. The very term, 'mystical' experience, seems a bit much. Looming above everything else as the decisive instance, there now stands a notable psychological prudence in Ignatius, the director, and the exercitant. It is that prudence that will discover the best service to God that can be expected of a subject who, in circumstances marked by great authenticity, *feels and understands a certain way* as he ponders his life in the light of Christ's life.

In the very next chapter we shall see that this eventuality, which might look like a 'mythical' or 'mystical' exaggeration on the part of Ignatius, actually provides us with a crucial christological datum, perhaps the most positive christological datum to be found in the Exercises.

Here, however, I want to offer some comments that might be regarded as criticisms of its claims. When we look at it from this standpoint, the first thing that surprises us is that whenever Ignatius defines or describes 'consolation', he almost always includes its character as a positive criterion of divine communication. Note the following: "I call it consolation when an interior movement is aroused in the soul, by which *it is inflamed with love of its Creator and Lord*, and as a consequence, can love no creature on the face of the earth *for its own sake*, but only in the Creator of them all. It is likewise consolation when one sheds tears that move to the love of God, whether it be because of sorrow for sins, or because of the sufferings of Christ our Lord, or for any other reason that is *immediately directed to the praise and service of God*. Finally, I call consolation every increase of faith, hope, and love, and all interior joy that invites and attracts to what is heavenly and *to the salvation of one's soul* by filling it with peace and quiet in its Creator and Lord" (316).[79]

My long citation has an incidental purpose as well: to remind my readers of the *test*-theology that is evident in this brief paraphrase of the First Principle and Foundation. But its main importance lies in the fact that if it is taken literally, it would logically render useless and pointless any 'discernment' with respect to movements in which such characteristics could be detected.

Once again we see Ignatius moving back to a much more ambiguous realm, where the criterion has to go by way of the psychological prudence of the director. Remember that consolation *without previous cause* is an unmistakable manifestation of the good spirit, i.e., of God. But, writes Ignatius: "*If a cause precedes*, both the good angel and the evil spirit can *give consolation* to a soul, but for a quite different purpose" (331).

But in that case, what is left of the above cited definition *as a criterion*? Nothing, it seems. And I say, 'it seems', because the psychological prudence of the director and the growing psychological experience of the exercitant in these contests of spirit will recognize whether the concrete consolation in question does or does not approach that valuational definition.

Even though that may salvage the logic, however, what now emerges as the criterion is the word used adjectivally three times in the last two paragraphs: *psychology*. The Rules for the Discernment of Spirits are actually a little manual of applied psychology, intuitive in approach but brilliant for their time and for having been worked out on the basis of real-life experience. Examining these rules one by one, any reader will see that their obvious *rationale* is psychological. In other words, with them we learn to know whether a concrete consolation fits the positive definition of consolation that Ignatius provides; and we do this by recognizing the psychological mechanisms involved and, through them, *what a given consolation is leading us to*. The same holds true for a concrete desolation.

There is nothing wrong with that. But it does tell us that there isn't any *theological* criterion above and beyond the two we have been studying. God does not communicate directly to the soul what service and praise God expects of it. During the Exercises, a sort of interior fencing match, psychological knowledge tells each 'knight' how far his offering can go, what exactly is the best service that God can expect of him, and hence, his authentic vocation. Teaching him to know himself and his latent spiritual capabilities, it tells him how far he can carry the imitation of Christ: or, to put it better, how far greater imitation is compatible with the greater praise and service of the Divine Majesty.

More than anything else, the theme of demythologization has helped us to recognize once again the same theology and christology (both as present and absent) that we have been encountering from the start. But I think it has also enabled us to see more clearly that the Exercises are moving toward something else. Toward what? Toward an ultimate criterion that Ignatius may have found in his own life, but that he could not formulate logically and consistently in the Exercises within the theological framework of his age: i.e., the objective criterion of the 'greater service of God our Lord'.

CHAPTER VI

King—Kingdom—Reign

I

From the previous chapters it should be clear to my readers that we find a real ambiguity in the Exercises. That ambiguity has to do with more or less the same point, although we have come across it by going down different pathways.

It seems, for example, that the notion of 'service' does not quite fit in with the conception of a test, although logically it should. It seems that 'indifference', which obviously is connected with one's subjective freedom of choice, should link up and disappear with the ultimate criterion of the test faced by the human being. Instead, however, it persists in dependence on an abstract criterion even after the example of Christ has been considered, awaiting a further criterion of a rather mysterious nature: Does God want me for this imitation or not? It then seems that this last criterion comes down to an immediate divine communication to the creature, indicating the specific, personal service expected of the latter. But this criterion, which is 'demythologized' in the Exercises themselves, looks an awful lot like what we today would call a *vocational test*, one that is taken with the help of concrete personal experiences that are interpreted by psychology.

In every chapter, in other words, we find loose threads that are intimately interrelated and that point toward a more developed christology than the one we examined in Chapter III.

To develop or work out such a christology, we can start from either one of two possible christological extremes: i.e., christology from *above* or christology from *below*. At one end of the spectrum a christology from above tells us that we come to know the Father and his love only through the living testimony of the Son. At the other end of the spectrum a christology from below would begin with the same theme that Jesus of Nazareth used in beginning his public ministry in Galilee: the kingdom of God is at hand.

If we start at either christological end and move carefully toward the other, we shall come up with a christology that is richer, more profound, and perhaps more suited to the intent of the Ignatian Exercises than the one Ignatius expresses in terms of a theology wherein the human being is being *tested* by the law and helped by the *example* of Christ, God Incarnate.

Let us briefly try to go down these two pathways. Or, to put it better, let us try to travel this one road from both ends. Let us begin with christology from above. 'God is love', writes the Johannine author, summing up people's actual experience of Jesus of Nazareth. As the author of the First Letter of John demands, let us give up the idea of evaluating love on the basis of our presuppositions about the essence of God. Let us do the opposite, instead: try to know God on the basis of *our own experience* of what love is (1 Jn 4:8). For example, it is impossible to conceive of a love where the lover would remain 'indifferent' to the decisions and destiny of the person loved. Therefore, it must be 'different' for God when a human being decides to love or hate a brother. We understand that 'difference' when we see someone laying down his life so that love may be a real possibility, a 'life', in our existence endowed with freedom (1 Jn 3:15–16; 4:9–10).

But we must go further. To love is to entrust something of one's own, something that is crucial for us, to the freedom of the person we love. Otherwise we will regard that person merely as an object. And note further that this love cannot be merely individual, since we human beings are affected in our lives and decisions by factors that lie outside us and that are also human beings with social structures linking us and them.

Now if we cannot live without entrusting something crucial of our own to others, then obviously we cannot truly love someone unless we share a common *project* with that person, a project that is important both to that person and ourselves. And since no project can be merely individual, as we just noted, to say that God is love is to say that God makes the human being an indispensable collaborator in, and crucial creator of, a project that is of the utmost importance both to God and the human being.[80]

That such a project may and does exist in fact is proved, for example, by the criterion God will use to judge the nations (Mt 25:31f.). Everything we do for the least of our brothers and sisters immediately affects God, who, without the slightest trace of egotism, loves those persons.

Suddenly we see that the fact that God is love, a fact derived from christology, leaves behind any conception of human existence as a *test*. It plants us before a common human and divine *project* that is unfolding in the history of human beings and their dire needs.

If we start from the other end of christology, we see appearing in Galilee an ordinary human being whose sole interest, in the eyes of his contemporaries, is to announce that 'the time is at hand' for God to implement His project, i.e., His kingdom. Whatever one's opinion about its eschatological proximity may be, that project signifies notable changes in reality as it was perceived by the people of that day. The first thing we learn from Jesus is that the kingdom will entail the happiness of the poor, to whom it is directed in order to change their unjust plight, and the disgrace or misfortune of the rich, whose project has already been fulfilled by the advantages and satisfactions they have gotten in the present reality that is going to be destroyed (Lk 6:20–26). With this new project in mind, Jesus of Nazareth calls the Twelve to be with him. He will send them out to preach, by word and deed, the conflict-ridden news of the arrival of the kingdom (Mk 3:14; Mt 10:7).

The *historical* nature of this project shows up mainly in two elements that have been brought out by exegesis and that we examined in Volume II of this series. Close study of the redaction of Matthew's and Luke's Gospels permits us to conclude that the original three Beatitudes were addressed to the poor as such, not because they were pious or 'poor in spirit'. The first concern of the new king in ushering in his reign reflects a clear preference for all those who have been objects of scorn, injustice, and marginalization, whether they are good or bad. The second element is the fact that this preference of God's for the poor does not lead Jesus to make himself even poorer but rather to introduce a terrible *conflict* into Israel by shouldering the cause of the poor. The 'good news' is for the poor; it is not directly or immediately for everyone. In its historical setting, in fact, it is 'bad news' for those who already have had their reward in the present regime or kingdom. And there is one important item: the unleashing of this conflict in the name of God's preferences will lead Jesus of Nazareth to confrontation, then suffering, and then death on a cross. Jesus lives the cross as a failure, undoubtedly a necessary failure, not as a goal or final purpose (Mt 26:38 and parallel texts; Mt 27:46 and parallel texts).

Before proceeding further, let us try to draw some conclusions from this incipient christology.

The *first*, logically, is the destruction of the concept of test as a description or definition of human existence before God. This entails a radical correction of Ignatius's First Principle and Foundation, because the latter can no longer be based merely on the Creator-creature relationship.

It is the precise and proper function of christology to pull us out of any such relationship and introduce us to personal intimacy with the Father. Paul repeatedly states this (Rom 8:15–16; Gal 4:4–6), declaring that we are no longer under the criterion of the Law, i.e., of a *test*.[81]

Given this christology, can we say that anything valid remains in Ignatius's First Principle and Foundation? The logical answer would seem to be 'no', but I have already called attention to the ambiguity of the word 'service' at this point in the Ignatian Exercises and throughout.

We saw that Ignatius's use of the term can mean mere obedience to the law; but we also saw that it somehow remains as a loose thread as well, since the term 'service' ordinarily implies a plan, a project, a historical interest and fits that formulation of the issue better than the notion of a test. We also noted that once what is commanded and what is prohibited have been recognized, and once the imitation of the model represented by the Son of God has been carried as far as the third kind of humility, service reappears as a mysterious, higher criterion.

The logic of the christology we are pursuing here would prompt us to replace the First Principle and Foundation with a corrected version of the call of the eternal King, which, readers will recall, is half of the parable of the Call of an Earthly King. The vocation of the human being is not decided by the creature-Creator relationship in the absence of christology, but by some possible objective service to a historical plan that we must call 'kingdom' and that Jesus introduced into history, establishing its fundamental criteria in the process.

Hence we need a *corrected* version of the Ignatian meditation on the eternal King. We saw earlier that the project of the king—both the earthly king and the eternal King—was not really specified or individualized. Stress was laid on the parallel and detailed following of the king in all the difficulties and sufferings demanded by the undertaking. The case is very different with the christology we are discussing here. The (Christian) human being is created to *serve* a historical project with concrete criteria and preferences. Living in circumstances different from those of the king, the Christian human being, rather than imitating, will have to create equally different strategies, but ones that ever remain in line with the objective criteria of the kingdom. It is *by this means* that the kingdom will be established, since the will of the king will begin to take actual effect on earth as it does in heaven (Mt 6:10).

So we get a new version of the meditation on the eternal King as the First Principle and Foundation. In this new version emphasis shifts from *king* to *kingdom*, i.e., to the plans, criteria, and preferences that characterize it, and ultimately from kingdom to *reign*,[82] i.e., to the concrete, creative introduction of those criteria into real history.

The *second* consequence of our incipient christology has to do with the function and use of created things. To be sure, they have been created for human beings, to help them achieve their goal. But when we shift from a test-theology to a christology of God's reign, a profound change takes place in the help that things give to human beings.

In the test-theology, 'things' have two characteristics that are not really intimately interconnected. On the one hand, they display in themselves some sort of value or attraction that arouses human desire or preference. On the other hand, a law from God inscribes in these things commandments or prohibitions that prescind from the desire they may arouse in human beings. It also seems that the test is clearer when the label 'no' is put on things that naturally arouse greater preference in human beings. So we gradually discover that God puts more value on those things to which the human being is not spontaneously drawn or attached.

At the stage of the First Principle and Foundation, however, we still know nothing about any such divine preferences. We do know from experience that things attract us, and that they distract us from the test by virtue of the attachment they cause. Since we do not know whether the label 'commanded', 'prohibited', or 'indifferent' will be on things when we meet them in the concrete, it is obvious that any attachment prior to knowing the criterion is *inordinate* and has to be combatted.

Our incipient christology, the absence of which we note precisely at the start of the Exercises (i.e., in the First Principle and Foundation and the First Week), radically transforms this conception. Right away, things in themselves lose their labels deriving from some law external to human beings and pre-existent to their projects (Mk 7:14–23). Now things become *useful* or *counterproductive* (1 Cor 6:12; 10:23) with respect to the divine and human project of establishing the reign of God in the world, a world where there will be an ever-increasing amount of love and its attendant conditions: freedom, justice, solidarity, equality, and communication.

Thus, a shift from fear of things to lordship over them must be an essential part of any First Principle and Foundation, if the latter is to dovetail with an essential datum of christology: i.e., our status as children of God and our consequent freedom vis-à-vis the law so that we will be able to offer our creative collaboration to the establishment of God's reign.

The least we can say is that this 'spiritual' experience of divine adoption as child of God, which is central for Paul (Rom 8:14–17), is neither contemplated nor projected in the unfolding of the Spiritual Exercises. Yet everything depends on it: (fiducial) *faith*, first of all, which makes love possible by liberating the human being from anxiety over its own plight and destiny. The 'salvation of my soul', which ever remains the essential concern of the Ignatian Exercises, is something I can forget about and leave in God's hands: not to lapse into some form of passivity that waits for the gift of justice from on high, but to shoulder the creative responsibility of 'living for others' (Rom 14:7.20–23). Both the Reformation (even in the profound spiritual experience of Luther) and the Counter Reformation were too preoccupied with salvation, the justifying decree of God, and predestination to notice the anthropological purpose and point that Paul attributes to faith. As we saw in Volume III, that purpose and point is to liberate human creativity from egotistical anxiety over a *test* and direct it toward a creative use of the universe.

In the spirituality of the Ignatian Exercises the universe never belongs to human beings as it should according to christology, Paul's christology at least. That is why *fear* and *love* constitute two stages, one more perfect than the other, in the correct use of creatures (370, 65), not two opposing attitudes as they are for Paul (Rom 8:15; Gal 5:4–6; see also 1 Jn 4:18). Carrying on the call to construct the reign of God under the aegis of grace, on the other hand, presupposes uprooting all traces of personal anxiety for ourselves (Lk 12:22–32).

The *third* consequence of our incipient christology has to do with another one of the loose threads in the lively logic of the Ignatian Exercises: i.e., the indifference, or better, the 'making ourselves indifferent' of the First Principle and Foundation.

There indifference is the rational consequence of the fact that things are means, and hence should be used *insofar as* they lead us to our goal or end. Every notion of valuing them or having an attachment to them for what they are in themselves has to be considered 'inordinate', since it prevents our will from using them freely.

At first glance it might seem that locating this end in a test based on law or in a historical project should not really have any effect on this 'insofar as' that measures the use of creatures, and hence on the indifference needed to avoid inordinate attachment to any one of them.

But there is a major difference here. The test does not give any definitive value of its own to any thing. The only thing that has value of its own is the result of the test, i.e., salvation, which *in itself* does not have any relation to the thing in question either. For example, if I choose 'poverty with Christ poor rather than riches' or 'insults with Christ loaded with them rather than honors', the salvific result will not be the continuation or multiplication of poverty and insults but just the opposite: the wealth and honor of the 'victory', which completely reverses the situation of one's 'labors', just as the 'suffering' chosen is converted into 'glory' (167, 93, 95).

Since there is no intrinsic relationship between means and end, not the slightest amount of the emotion or enthusiasm I can invest in the end can be transferred to the means. I must wait and hope in 'indifference' for the means to be indicated to me. This shows up clearly in many parts of the Exercises, but especially in the first way of choosing in the third 'time of tranquillity': "It is necessary to keep as my aim the end for which I am created, that is, *the praise of God our Lord and the salvation of my soul*. Besides this, I must be *indifferent*, without any *inordinate* attachment, so that I am not more inclined or disposed to accept the object in question than to relinquish it, nor to give it up than to accept it. I should be like a balance at equilibrium, without leaning to either side, that I might be ready to follow whatever I perceive [*sintiere*] is more for the glory and praise of God our Lord and for the salvation of my soul" (179).

My readers will note that in this passage indifference is expressed and required in the present, whereas leaving it through knowledge of the means most appropriate to the end has a *future* cast: *sintiere*. This difference in time is another characteristic feature of the test-situation. Looking at the essence of a thing, I cannot lean toward a yes or no. Any such leaning would be inordinate. *Once* I know or perceive where God is placing the test, *then and only then* can I move out of indifference.

We have already seen how this strange sequence is repeated over and over again. It occurs first at the level of the law, as if the face of the earth were covered with creatures toward which the logical human attitude would be one of calculation. Then, once commanded and prohibited things have been eliminated, indifference and the 'insofar as' calculus dominate the rest of the universe until the imitation of Christ reveals where God wants to test us by pointing out to us God's unsuspected preferences. Finally, however, even this criterion is left in suspense and is once again to be dominated by indifference and calculation, since even the imitation of Christ is, in every case, subordinated to a criterion of service that is difficult to determine and closely bound up with choosing a way of life. This ultimate criterion once again imposes indifference and calculation.

Now in a project-christology, such as that centered around the reign of God on earth, it is true that the 'insofar as' in the use of things and its associated indifference do enter the picture. But here their function is totally different, for two obvious reasons.

The first reason is that any authentically historical project, such as that of the reign of God, entails valuing certain persons and concrete things from the very start and then transforming reality to bring it in line with that prior valuation. As we saw in Volume II, in other words, a project like the reign of God entails general *preferences* that clearly direct our 'attachment', from the very start, to specific things and person. A *prior* indifference—such as that of the Pharisees, who specifically espoused a test-theology—would make a person deaf to the call of the king. Only after the preference does indifference have a place and meaning as the capacity to choose the best means for carrying out the project. Thus, indifference is identified with objectivity, and the latter with effectiveness.

The second reason why the function of things is different here is that the force which makes indifference possible is precisely the preference: i.e., one's concrete enthusiasm for the project and the specific 'things' it contains. This is the case rather than vice versa. I can 'make myself indifferent' only *after* and *because* I feel enthusiasm for a historical purpose and goal. I cannot work up enthusiasm for an abstract criterion that does not entail preferences for concrete things or persons. I cannot work up enthusiasm for the praise of God or the salvation of my soul if I am not already enthusiastic for concrete things and persons that will be affected by both. Hence this sort of enthusiasm for an abstract criterion raises the suspicion that a person is, at bottom, thinking of something else but, instead of calling it by name, for some unknown reason prefers to give it an abstract label that is hard to associate with concrete projects. Remember the clear warning of the First Letter of John: "If anyone says, 'I love God', and yet hates his brother, he is a *liar*; for whoever does not love his *brother whom he sees cannot love God whom he does not see*" (1 Jn 4:20). One cannot deny that indifference, as it is described in the Ignatian Exercises, seems to be linked to the suspicion of an interior lie.

As I shall try to show later on in this volume, there can be no doubt whatsoever that Ignatius Loyola, not to mention others, understood and interpreted indifference *otherwise* in his own life. But there can also be no doubt that he, within the framework of the theology of his age, was unable to give it the spiritual expression that his solidly historical conception of the divine project would have called for. He was not the first mystic who, in trying to express himself, did not find the appropriate terms in the contemporary theology of the Church.

I said above that in the light of a more profound christology the First Principle and Foundation should to some extent be replaced by the call of the eternal King, insofar as the destiny of the human being is concerned. And I would also insist that it would have to be a corrected version of the call of the eternal King. Now, insofar as indifference to created things is concerned, we conclude that the First Principle and Foundation should to some extent be replaced by a version of the Meditation on Two Standards, taking the word 'standard' in its metaphorical sense of *project*, which is already present in the Exercises. Again, I am talking about a corrected version. Instead of discussing the *virtues* required for the service of the Commander in Chief, this reworked version would offer a properly christological exposition of the content and goal of the *historical* project known as the reign of God.

II

Christology is also compelled to step in and abet a new and important reorientation within the overall process of the Ignatian Exercises: i.e., the suppression of the First Week.

Traditional as it may be to assume that the purgative way should precede the illuminative way, it is obvious that no Christian theology of sin exists outside of christology. In the preceding chapters we have seen that the christological vacuum—not only implicit but also explicit— extends from the first Principle and Foundation to the first contemplation of the Second Week. So it is logical to assert, in principle, that the contemplations on Christ will explain to us the real sense, importance, and presence of sin.

Furthermore, in the previous section we specifically dealt with the need to include in the First Principle and Foundation some meditations that recapitulate, in some way, what Christ taught about the reign of God by word and deed. I mentioned specifically the Call of an Earthly King and the Meditation on Two Standards. It would be completely illogical now to go back and examine what sin is without taking into account the human destiny made manifest by Jesus Christ when he revealed to us, in his person, the mystery of the Father and His active, plan-oriented love. Only a profound union with Jesus and his objectives can prompt us, when we consider his persistent and growing opposition to his enemies and their 'hour' as he hangs on the cross, to feel sorrow for our sins and finally realize what they really are.

In saying this, I am not passing judgment on the 'psychological' effectiveness of the First Week. I do not claim to know whether, in the majority of exercitants, starting with an understanding of the Christian project can match the shock one experiences in the First Week when one ponders sin as something isolated (52,58), shameful (48,74), antinatural (57,58,60), and related solely to its culmination: hell. In a spirituality, however, what is effective cannot go against what is theological, what comes down to a deeper and more solid understanding of the faith. And if it is demonstrated that the christology of the Exercises and Ignatius's age must be regarded *today* as defective or incomplete, then we will have to give up a First Week in which christology is not present.

I myself must abide by the same logic, to be sure. I cannot criticize the conception of sin expounded in the First Week until I have examined the christological data that surfaces in an analysis of the Second Week. Here I can only offer three preliminary observations that are along the lines of those made in the previous section.

First: in the test-theology, the conception of sin is strictly individual. Each human being is judged, alone, before the law. In a christology of God's reign, by contrast, every sin becomes social as the project itself is. That is to say, every fault or sin poses an obstacle to the reign of God and consequently causes harm to its beneficiaries.

Second: anxiety over the salvation of one's own soul paralyzes the human being, or at least diminishes its creativity with respect to any project, since not acting is the safest way to avoid violating the law. This is all the more true since the law in question here, like any law, is more precise and clear about what it prohibits than what it commands. The meaning of the precept, 'Thou shalt not kill', for example, is much more obvious than would be the meaning of a precept, 'Thou shalt fight for the lives of your fellow human beings'. The obvious consequence, then, is that a person can keep all the commandments without loving: the only explanation consistent with the gospel incident where eternal life is denied to a person who can claim to have observed all the commandments (Lk 18:18–27). This sin of omission will increasingly grow more important and crucial than any and all voluntary sins insofar as society depends on increasingly complex mechanisms that operate (and even kill) by themselves.

Third: in the teaching of Jesus, the biggest sinner is the person who makes use of and fulfills the law for his or her own peace or security of conscience. This will lead such a person, wittingly or unwittingly, to turn the law into a criterion or instrument for oppressing those who, for one reason or another, have been unable to fulfill it (Lk 18:9–14).

I don't think I am being unfair to the Ignatian Exercises when I say that these three dimensions of sin, essential to the gospel message (at least in the eyes of present-day christology), are absent from the First Week. They could not possibly be present there since only contemplations dealing with Christ and his project for the reign of God, with its consequent vision of sin, could reveal them.

That prompts me to take a closer look at the central week of the Ignatian Exercises: the Second Week. I have already indicated the sort of correction I would suggest for the Call of an Earthly King, shifting from the theme of imitation to that of project. I said the same thing with regard to the Meditation on Two Standards. That sort of correction would go hand in hand with the logical shift of those two meditations to the section devoted to the end and destiny of the human being: i.e., the First Principle and Foundation.

So I am now left with the task of offering a few observations on the Ignatian contemplation of the Incarnation, the three kinds of humility, and the process of choosing a way of life.

Christologically speaking, we find it difficult to define or describe the purpose of the Incarnation. It is especially difficult to do so before we know how the witnesses of Jesus of Nazareth themselves interpreted it: i.e., how, from what they saw and heard of Jesus, they arrived at the conclusion that he was God Incarnate and then ended up, if so they did, determining the overall purpose of the Incarnation.

This, in fact, is the only Ignatian contemplation which, at least in the section on the divine persons that precedes the Annunciation to Mary, does not have a biblical or gospel passage in its history. I am not considering the various Ignatian 'parables' here, of course.

In this contemplation the exercitant is to "see and consider the Three Divine Persons seated on the royal dais or throne of the Divine Majesty. They look down upon the whole surface of the earth, and behold all nations in great blindness, going down to death and descending into hell" (106). Then the exercitant is to "hear what the Divine Persons say, that is, 'Let us work the redemption of the human race', etc." (107). Finally, the exercitant is to consider "what the Divine Persons do, namely, work the most holy Incarnation" (108).

Now it is certainly true that each of the relatively elaborate writings in the New Testament presents a christology of its own, and that it is not easy to harmonize them all. The christologies of the Synoptic Gospels, for example, are not the same, even though they contain similar elements. The individuality and originality of Paul, John, and the author of the Apocalypse are even clearer.

It is also true that Ignatius's contemplation on the Incarnation—at least with respect to the point noted above about the relation of test and project—bears some resemblance to the christology elaborated in the Letter to the Hebrews. At first glance, its vocabulary and use of the term 'Incarnation' might lead us to surmise that the christological influence comes from the fourth Gospel, but the resemblance actually goes no further. Even though the Letter to the Hebrews does not offer such an all-embracing christology, it has more points of structural contact with the conception of the Incarnation in the Ignatian Exercises and, of course, with the theology of Ignatius's age.

It is not a literal influence but a significant one, and there is something quite paradoxical about it all. In its own day the Letter to the Hebrews was a radical critique of cultic worship in the Old Testament, which, said its author, had been abolished once and for all by and in Christ. Yet, more than any other New Testament writing, the Letter to the Hebrews came to serve as a bridge between the Old Testament and the New Testament with respect to the matter of cultic worship specifically.

To be sure, various New Testament writings—e.g., those of Paul—speak of redemption; others, such as the Johannine writings, speak of the incarnation. And there is no doubt that the two notions are brought together in some of the christological hymns we find in Paul's letters dating from his period of imprisonment (Eph 1:3–14; Col 1:15–20). But no other author in the New Testament resembles the author of the Letter to the Hebrews in elaborating a christology based almost exclusively on the cultic themes of temple, redemption, priesthood, a new covenant sealed in blood offered up in sacrifice, mediation, and so forth (Heb 1:1–3; 2:10; 4:1–3; 5:5–9; 9:12–15; 10:5–7; etc.).

In the Letter to the Hebrews the unique priesthood of Christ, linked to his twofold condition as God and human being, is presented as a complement to the test-theology (Heb 12:2). We needed someone, divine in propitiatory power but experientially knowledgeable about our frailty before the law (Heb 4:14–5:1), who could offer God a redemptive sacrifice for our sins. Jesus did that when he shed his blood on the cross (Heb 5:3).

This christology, already independent of its literary source in many instances, grew and developed for centuries in Christendom and became, paradoxically enough, the clearest basis for the annual cycle of the Christian liturgy.[83]

The problem for the Spiritual Exercises was that this christology, taken out of the historical context where it was created and where it made complete sense, made it difficult for people to comprehend more important christological data: e.g., Jesus' stress on the arrival of the kingdom and its consequences. In spite of the Call of the Earthly King, then, in the Exercises of Ignatius the Incarnation does not seem to be associated with a historical project: the reign of God. Instead it seems to be a very belated attempt to solve another problem: i.e., the fact that the conditions of the test were so unfavorable to human beings that they were ending up in hell, except for rare exceptions (106).

This sacrificial view of the Incarnation will take on crucial importance in the Three Kinds of Humility, the second point I wish to consider in the Second Week. I have already indicated that Ignatius's choice of the word 'humility' to designate the *abstract* criterion of every choice is a bit of a surprise and probably highly significant. In the first kind of humility it is described as 'submission': "It consists in this, that as far as possible I so *subject and humble myself*" (165) as to accept a divine criterion inscribed in things completely independent of me.[84]

A less likely second hypothesis is that the term is taken from the third kind of humility and characterizes the second criterion, the one that comes after the law of God: i.e., the greater imitation of Christ. Ignatius writes: "I desire and choose poverty with Christ poor . . . insults with Christ loaded with them; . . . I desire to be accounted as worthless and a fool for Christ. . . . So Christ was treated before me" (167). This picture of Christ could be summed up in the word 'humility'.

In the first hypothesis we note the presence of a test-theology as opposed to a project-christology. In the context of a test, the human being *is worthless before God*. The only thing the human being can do, then, is accept the imposition of a criterion that is alien to its desires and supposed personal importance. Merit is the thing of value. The person as such has no value; it is merely the precondition required for the test. Nothing of this changes in the third kind of humility, with its criterion of the greatest possible imitation of Christ. In the Call of an Earthly King it was already clear that my collaboration was not desired because I was important in the fulfillment of the king's project. His enterprise simply offered me a chance to 'distinguish' myself in imitating him so that, as the king puts it, "by following me in suffering, he may follow me in glory" (95).

In this connection we do well to recall what we saw in Volume III. Paul's christology destroys the vertical scheme echoed by Ignatius here: God—law—human being. Paul replaces that scheme with the properly Christian one: God—human being—law. Note Paul's statements about the law (Gal 3:10.22.23.25; 4:2–5.21.26; 5:18), and his corresponding statements about ownership (1 Cor 3:21–23) that turn the follower of Christ into God's co-worker (*synergos*) in the divine project that Paul metaphorically describes as 'planting' or 'building' (1 Cor 3:8–9).

In a spirituality this difference in attitude and approach is crucial, not to say worlds apart. I hardly need stress the necessity of choosing between them. As Paul himself sees it, nothing less than Christian existence itself is at stake.

The second hypothesis, that humility refers to the attitude of Christ who is to be imitated, does not really alter the first insofar as the test-theology is concerned. If one prefers it, there is no essential change in perspective. Imitation is a way, more human perhaps but at bottom the same, of using an impersonal, external criterion and subjecting the personal to it.

As we saw in Chapter III of this volume, however, such an approach falsifies the history of Jesus himself as we know it. He was not the model of poverty in the society of his own day, as is evident from the way he is compared unfavorably to John the Baptist (Mt 11:18–19). And summing up his life as a series of insults from adversaries who regard him as a fool is either a plain mistake or a false perspective due to focusing solely on his passion. Jesus' life was more uncomfortable than poor (compare, e.g., Lk 8:1–3 with Lk 9:57–58), and more conflict-ridden than ignominious. Moreover, both features are framed within a purpose or project, as are the pain and suffering of his passion.

The huge christological vacuum in this kind of humility, which seems to succumb to a predilection for suffering or masochism, lies in the failure to notice that in the real life of Jesus there is not the slightest indication that suffering was valued for its own sake. Death, which Christ 'barely' accepts, was the price he had to pay for the values he advocated and defended, and more specifically, for his determination to bring happiness to the poor, sinners, and the marginalized members of society, who constituted one and the same group. That is inexcusably left out of account in the third kind of humility as Ignatius presents it; and, as we shall see, this complicates the final criterion to be used in choosing a way of life.

That brings me to the third point that we must consider in the Second Week of the Ignatian Exercises: the method of making a choice about a way of life. At first glance, as we saw earlier, it seems inappropriate to talk about 'ways' of making a choice after the concrete precautions of the Three Classes of Men and the general christological criteria of the Three Kinds of Humility. Everything seems to be already provided, so that no more indications or guidelines are needed.

That is not the case, however. Ignatius's cautious supplement, together with the Rules for the Discernment of Spirits, shows us precisely the point where all our loose threads converge: i.e., in a personal service which seems to detach itself from any test-theology, and in which indifference ceases to keep the person unattached to things and persons because he or she now confronts the ultimate criterion of God's will that is beyond even the imitation of Christ. We now glimpse the outlines or beginnings of a divine plan wherein each individual human being can and should discover the best and indispensable service it can offer to God our Lord.

I might also note that the Three Times When a Correct and Good Choice May Be Made also represent as many loose threads, some of them ambiguous, the others without much logical relationship to the criteria derived from the Ignatian contemplations or meditations. We noticed the extraordinary and quasi-miraculous first time, Ignatius's mistrust of the time of tranquillity and the rational use of criteria received from meditations, and the ambiguity of the discernment deriving from consolations or desolations. The discernment seemed to fluctuate between mystical experience and common-sense psychological criteria, while the consolations and desolations seemed to be independent of the Exercises being undertaken. All these things suggest that the definitive and ultimate criterion points to a different world, one that was glimpsed by Ignatius but not explicitly reached in the Exercises insofar as theological expression was concerned.

As I see it, this point of convergence is a project-christology, the one we have been approaching by the *via negativa* in this chapter. All the Ignatian loose threads come together in the reign of God on earth that Jesus preached and inaugurated, and all the ambiguities of the Ignatian presentation thereby fade away.

We have seen that already with respect to the points prior to choosing a way of life. Now let us see how it shows up with respect to that essential point.

Perhaps the clearest consequence of shifting from a test-theology to a project-christology is the difference in the ultimate criterion of one's choice. Anxiety over avoiding a mistake in a test (lack of faith, in Paul's sense) prompts people to seek out atemporal, infallible criteria. In the Synoptic Gospels, this is the key to the characteristic theology of the Pharisees and the 'choice' they make regarding Jesus. They demand a 'sign of heaven' (Mk 8:11–12; Mt 12:38–42; 16:1–4; Lk 11:29; 12:54–57).

These kinds of signs as criteria for making a decision inevitably remind us of the ways of choosing that are described in the Ignatian Exercises, and of the search for the final, ultimate criterion in particular. In responding to the Pharisees, however, Jesus himself puts the stress on the 'signs of the times': i.e., those signs which, once God's project has been made known and accepted, come to us from history itself and our knowledge of its objective possibilities. These signs are ambiguous and relative, to be sure; but they suffice for human affairs, as Jesus pointedly notes.

But perhaps the most noteworthy thing about the examples presented in the Gospels of people or groups who knew how to perceive such signs is that historical sensitivity to such signs does not come down to 'indifference'. Instead it entails a 'difference' or 'preference', a prior enthusiasm. It entails certain specific values that the reign of God seeks to introduce concretely into real history and that must be present if the signs are to 'signify' something. There can be no indifferent interpretation of the signs of the times. People are either filled with enthusiasm or scandalized by them: "John . . . sent word by his disciples and said to him, 'Are you he who is to come, or should we look for another?' Jesus answered them, 'Go and tell John what you hear and see. The blind see, the lame walk, lepers are cleansed, the deaf hear, the dead are raised up, and *the poor have the good news announced to them*; and blessed is the one who *is not scandalized in me*' " (Mt 11:2–6; Lk 11:14–22.31; etc.).

In a project-christology there is no proper room for additional criteria between enthusiasm for the reign of God and its values on the one hand and delicate, nuanced experiential knowledge of the possibilities offered by the times on the other (Mt 16:2–3; the Johannine concept of 'the hour', Jn 2:4 and passim).

But the human being is complex, and so are historical circumstances. When it is necessary to interpret the signs of the times in such cases, one must see clearly into oneself. One must know whether enthusiasm for certain things derives from the criteria of God's reign and the signs of the times or from the 'attachments' that sprout on the sly and in disguise out of such interests and opportunities. The Ignatian ways of making a choice are suitable for *such* occasions. His precautions in the Three Classes of Men and the Rules for the Discernment of Spirits now take on their full human, evangelical (Lk 14:25–33), and divine logic. So does 'indifference', understood as a real disposition to faithfully follow those criteria once they have been perceived and clarified. The loose threads are now woven together.

The only problem is that none of this seems to be in the Exercises. The best proof of this fact is the difficulty of tying the loose threads without a christology of the sort I have been describing. Such a christology is obviously missing from the Exercises, and we have seen what a radical transformation the Exercises would have to undergo in order to make room for it. So much of a transformation, in fact, that we cannot help but ask ouselves what would then be left, if anything, of the methodology, force, and mystique of the Ignatian Exercises.[85]

CHAPTER VII

Conclusion: The Tensions of a Christology

I think that the preceding chapters, devoted to analyzing the christology implicit in the Ignatian Exercises, have pointed up a noticeable ambivalence in that christology. But if I am not mistaken, this weakness or vacuum could also mark the start of its historical relevance, however negatively we may judge its usefulness for us today.

By way of conclusion, then, I would like to pinpoint the root and source of that duality. In so doing, I also hope to show that the spirituality—or spiritualities, if you will—of that age does incorporate a christological element destined to have further developments and consequences. Having gotten this far, I must first try to correct an impression I may have given my readers. I have several times referred to the tension that often exists, especially in a 'spirituality', between the original experience behind it and the theoretical theological molds into which it is then poured. That is certainly true of the Ignatian Exercises, as my whole treatment should have made clear. It is also true that some of that ambiguity is due to the overlapping of two historical stages of composition: Ignatius's personal experiences in the Manresa phase, and his study of formal theology in the Paris phase. But here I am trying to bring out something more than that: i.e., a greater complexity, with its strengths and deficiencies.

I have already suggested that the tension underlying the ambivalence of the Ignatian Exercises could be expressed in terms of a test-christology versus a project-christology. Both kinds are present and relevant in the two historical phases of Ignatius's life, however, so we cannot characterize the latter simply in terms of a shift from a predominantly experiential phase to a predominantly theological phase. We must go further and delve into a more complicated historical context.

Even as early as Ignatius's experiences in Manresa, for example, we find two influences at work. Convalescing at his manor from wounds received in the battle of Pamplona, Ignatius Loyola asks for 'books of chivalry' to while away his time. For him, as for any reader of his day, the key interest was provided by the projects and adventures. When such books could not be found, Ignatius settled for 'lives of the saints'. He read them as *sacred* books of chivalry, however. God, too, has his knights, with their corresponding projects and adventures. "If them, why not me?" thought Ignatius, and this was the key to his conversion.

It continued to be the inner prompting that drove him to Manresa, where he would prepare for this new adventure and keep vigil over the new arms of a project that was still vague, that called for forces and a choice. The result of this preparation would be set down in his little book of Exercises.

Already at Manresa, however, the *Imitation of Christ* by Thomas à Kempis was part of his spiritual baggage. To one unaware of its contents, the title might suggest the imitation of the knight *par excellence*, who inaugurated the kingdom of God on earth. In reality, however, the book reflects a monastic spirituality of despising the world and its creatures in order to join the Creator in lonely contemplation of the eternal.

If we follow Ignatius from Manresa to Paris, we see that the latter influence takes on a more directly theological tone, in line with his studies. But during that same period, we must not forget, Ignatius Loyola was also much more involved in another endeavor than he had been in Manresa: i.e., the programmatic preparation of a group of companions who, without abandoning contemplation, were pondering their future activity as a service or adventure in the cause of Christ.

From start to finish in his writing of the Exercises, then, Ignatius would be caught in tension: not only between his own personal experiences and their theoretical expression, but also between different, not readily compatible elements of his experience, which he was handed by his context rather than creating on his own.

Let me now try to give a brief overview of these various elements and orientations.

I

Our shift from the New Testament in the previous two volumes to the age of Ignatius in this volume really represents an enormous leap insofar as the content of christology is concerned. Christology in Ignatius's era lives in a totally different context, and it is shaped to serve that context. Those close to Jesus and his time, who elaborated the christologies of the New Testament, could hardly have imagined the context in which Ignatius lived.

This is not a historical study. My aim in this volume is solely to analyze the Ignatian Exercises as a further example of christological creation. So I cannot offer a full and balanced picture of the Christendom in which Ignatius lived, and which deeply affected his own christology as it appears in the Exercises. Four elements must be noted, however, so that we may somewhat understand the new context surrounding the Ignatian christology that we have been examining.

I would call the attention of my readers to the fact that these elements derive from the closing middle ages rather than from the Renaissance or the Counter

Reformation, the latter being the period when Ignatius was operative as the founder and superior general of the Society of Jesus. These medieval elements are quite important at the point when Ignatius is creating his Exercises. Due to the persistence of Islam in Spain right up to the end of the fifteenth century, that country retained some medieval traits a century after the Renaissance had blotted them out in other parts of Europe.

The *first* crucial element is the fact that Jesus Christ is no longer a focal point of tension and conflict, as he had been in real history. He is now the founder of the religion that grounds and justifies the established order of Western Europe, and he is the fundamental factor of cohesion that minimizes all conflict between Christians.

The *second* element is that this self-proclaimed Christian world ponders God, particularly in its official statements, in terms borrowed from a Greek philosophy that had been fashioned behind the back of biblical thinking as it is found in both the Old and New Testaments.[86] One of those Greek categories ends up with the already mentioned primacy of contemplation over action.

The *third* element, which at first glance might seem to contradict the previous one, is the deep and universal devotion of Ignatius's age to Jesus, especially Jesus in his passion. Indeed, one of the most authentic features of the period seems to be an emotion-filled contemplation of the cross and a spirituality that draws from it crucial consequences for Christian living, both in 'the world' and the religious life. By 'authentic' here, I mean representative of something deeply rooted in the culture, not necessarily a complete or flawless interpretation of the christological material. What we are dealing with is the result of a christology from above, which converts the conflict-ridden project of Jesus into an atemporal demonstration of the values that God wanted to impress upon us through His Son's accomplishment of our redemption.

The *fourth* and final element is the fact that even though Jesus Christ is the transcendent factor of cohesion for the 'Christian' world, his name is used to sponsor both defensive and offensive undertakings insofar as that world is menaced by internal divisions or external attacks. People go to war in his name and kill in defense of his faith, just as they legislate, govern, reward, and punish for the same reasons.

These all too brief comments are meant to dust the cobwebs of habit from our eyes, so that we can gauge the enormous contextual change that had taken place in the Western world since Jesus of Nazareth preached his message fifteen centuries earlier. Now let me try to relate these general traits of the age to my analysis of the Exercises in the previous chapters of this volume.

(1). We have noted some sort of 'christological vacuum' in the Exercises, all the more curious because the following of Jesus occupies three of the four weeks in the Exercises. It is not so much that the Exercises give less place than they should to christology, as we saw, but that they have succumbed to some of the dangers inherent in christologies from above. The basic temptation is to lose sight of the 'relativity' of the concrete history of Jesus of Nazareth. When one tries to give it meaning on the basis of a plan that starts wholly from the mind of God, the historical causes set in motion by Jesus lose their crucial character. They are turned into a kind of parable, from which one is supposed to draw a divine moral.

Without being original, Ignatius Loyola draws his moral in the third kind of humility. What God values in the human being is the reproduction of the physical and moral sufferings that characterize the life of the Son of God and bring it to its culmination: rejection by human beings and the redemptive sufferings of the passion. Thus, the most significant moment in Jesus' life is the moment when his history ceases, when he abandons the world and the world abandons him.

To some extent, however, the case of the Exercises is atypical, statistically speaking at least, as we shall see when we analyze subsequent elements. It is, if you will, an extreme and paradoxical consequence of the first element we noted above: i.e. the conversion of the conflict-ridden message of Jesus into a dominant religion which, at the same time and for the same reason, becomes the divine sanction for the established norms of the sociopolitical order in the medieval Western world.

For that to happen, the Christian Church had to be the only institution to survive the fall of the Roman Empire, to remain intact as the latter was besieged and finally overrun by the successive invasions of the peoples on its peripheries known as 'barbarians'.

Comparisons are useful, though never wholly adequate. So we could say that under the shield and authority of the Church there took place a new occupation of the 'promised land', a new civil and sedentary organization of primitive peoples who had previously been more or less nomadic and certainly pagan. The Church had to overcome in them the temptation to syncretism that was stirred, as once it had been in Canaan, by the brilliant fallen empire with its gods and goddesses and culture. And it had to overcome it with the very same ambiguous but indispensable weapon, intermingling rejection and acceptance in limited doses.

For good or ill, the Christian Church took on and carried out the functions of a Moses, a Joshua, a David, an Elijah, and so forth. It organized and civilized peoples in the name of Christ, as Israel had done earlier in the name of Yahweh. The only problem is that while the Church spoke the name of Christ, it actually returned to stages that clearly were of an Old Testament nature; basically, it returned to an anthropology based on the law.

In another work I expressed the opinion that the extraordinary and persistent influence exerted by Greek philosophy throughout the Middle Ages and even much later, on the academic level at the very least, could not be attributed solely to its intrinsic value or the more or less fortuitous historical circumstances of the West: e.g., the fortunate preservation and communication of the major works of that philosophy to the West, thanks to Arab culture.[87]

Its acceptance, in any case, was not fortuitous. Nor was it accidental that its representation of God as the transcendence of the order could not value human freedom in and of itself. The latter, in fact, enjoyed the curious privilege of being able to break that order. For the Christian and the citizen who really was such, freedom could only be the condition of a test. The use of freedom would be rewarded or punished, in the external forum by 'Christian' society and in the internal forum by the 'Christian' God.

Thus, central passages of Paul that were solidly rooted in the gospel message came to be overlooked or forgotten. I mean those passages that equated the Christian moment with the emergence of the human being from infancy and childhood into mature adulthood, where its creative freedom as a child of God was to redeem the world from its uselessness.

(2). But how could Christianity, with its call to the loftiest heroism and loving service to the brethren even unto death, agree to accept the social function— which was undoubtedly necessary—of serving as the 'pedagogue' of still infantile peoples, of human masses still looking for organization and law? How, in that situation, could Christianity keep rereading the message of Jesus every day and adapt itself to that infantile context, one that had become very much 'bourgeois', to use a significant anachronism?

In this connection it is very interesting to note that the first *practical* division in Christendom took place in the early centuries as soon as this tension between incompatible things was noticed. It was then that people sought 'the desert' and fled from 'Christian civilization' as it had taken solid shape, in cities primarily. The first hermits wanted to live Christianity and its heroic demands to the fullest.[88]

With the first hermits we get the birth of what would later be called 'spirituality' in the strictest sense. And the same motivating impulse would be apparent in the Ignatian Exercises centuries later, when the exercitant would be urged to ask for "a knowledge of the world, that filled with horror, I may put away from me all that is worldly and vain" (63).

Since there was no formal heterodoxy in this movement, it was gradually reabsorbed by the official Church as a level of *perfection* higher than that required of all.

Theoretically, the basis of this 'perfection' was considered to lie in the *contemplative life*. But what we know about the origins of the eremetic movement seems to suggest a much more direct relation to christology. More than anything else, it seems to have been a criticism of massification in the name of the heroism and conflictiveness associated with the following of Christ in the principal christologies of the New Testament.

In all likelihood, it was not the thought of tranquil contemplation but the notion of battle that drew anchorites to the desert. If one abandoned all compromise and entanglement with the facile reality of civilized life, it was assumed that the enemies who confronted Christ would appear in full force. Then would begin the real combat, without which Christianity loses its meaning. Disregarding the additional color added by imagination and art, we can say that the temptations of St. Anthony, the father of the anchorites, offer reliable cultural testimony of what people were seeking in the desert. Other similar kinds of testimony could be offered, of course.

In the geographical and theological recapture of the anchorites by official Christianity, it is clear that an important role was played in the medieval West by the theoretical primacy of the contemplative life over the active life.

However, it is difficult to imagine a division more alien to biblical thinking. As we have seen, it entails an anthropological conception that is clearly Greek. Not surprisingly, then, when Thomas Aquinas weighs the relative value of the two kinds of life and offers his central line of argument, which is usually biblical, he can find only one saying of Jesus that had traditionally been taken out of context.[89] His real reasons will be based, significantly, on 'the philosopher', i.e., Aristotle.[90]

Now this is far from being one of those academic questions of scholasticism that have been ridiculed and satirized by allusion to extreme examples: e.g., How many angels can fit on the head of a pin?

In a world prone to almost continual wars, invasions, and all sorts of crucial and pressing necessities, the priority of the contemplative life over the active life was quite alien to the real-life existence of the masses. It had to find its origin and justification in a specific conception of God. And since God revealed Self in Jesus, the further implication would be that there was a specific christology behind this strange 'division of labor'.[91]

The fact is that in Ignatius's time, and for some centuries before that, christology could not fully perform the function of giving any positive meaning to the active (Christian) life of lay people. Conceived 'from above', too hastily I think, it could only adapt itself to the idea of a God who, in the face of a world and a society structured by God, offered a *test* to human freedom. And to the Christian God also offered in Jesus the atemporal, ahistorical example of the surest and most perfect way to pass that test. Thus, by virtue of its context rather than by necessity, christology 'from above' came down to imitating Jesus *suffering* on the cross.

To be sure, the primacy of the contemplative life ('praising and reverencing God') clashed with too many things to impose itself completely. Later I shall examine the main breach in it, which would continue to widen as the Middle Ages waned. But its theoretical status was not even questioned. Similarly, Jesus was contemplated apart from his historical struggle and his temporal 'project'. This explains the ambiguity of the word 'service' (to God) that is so characteristic of the Ignatian Exercises.

(3). So we come to the third element, devotion to the crucified Jesus. On the one hand this might seem to be the very opposite of Greek philosophy insofar as the being of God is concerned. But we shall see that it is intimately connected with it, though from the perspective of popular piety.[92]

This devotion to the Crucified, to God crucified more precisely, derived from a christology from above, as I have already noted. At the level of the average Christian, however, it took on such strongly *realistic* traits that some theologians were led to the false conclusion that those traits derived from a christology from below or from an appreciation of the historical Jesus as he could have been known in his own day. That is the import of Ignatius's remarks and efforts to get the exercitant to contemplate Jesus 'as though present'.

It is the same christology from above that prevailed in academic theology, but without the theoretical 'purification' introduced by Greek metaphysics. The 'linguistic communication' affirmed by the early Councils was fully lived, but in the wrong direction somehow. It was not the historical Jesus who revealed to us what God is, but rather God who revealed to us the *hidden* significance of Jesus and his history.

The ministry and message of Jesus, with their inherent conflictiveness, were minimized, or translated into an atemporal moral teaching along the lines of Matthew's Gospel. The redemptive cross became the goal toward which the life of Jesus was directed, and the point from which his history took on definitive meaning. That was the plan of God. Depending on one's emphasis, Jesus' resurrection was a proof of his divinity or a reward for successfully passing the *test*: i.e., his obedience to his Father.

But the significance of Jesus lies in the fact that he carried out the Father's plan, the redemption of human beings, on the cross. God sent His own Son to suffer and die on a cross. Thus stripped of their historical causality and import, Jesus' suffering and death appear as a value-judgment, from the standpoint of the Absolute, regarding what is truly worthwhile in human existence. God suffered and died for us, so suffering and death are almost divinized. They constitute the object of our freedom, as in the third kind of humility in the Ignatian Exercises.

Average Christians, then, will experience the consolation they need in the face of their own suffering and death. Christians 'on the path of perfection' will try to 'make offerings of greater value', associating their contemplation of suffering with real-life suffering as a positive element in an existence undergoing a test. Christian contemplation, then, will not have the quality of 'apathy' that was associated with contemplation in the Greek view.

In this connection it is worth noting what we saw in the verses of Jorge Manrique, for example. As a man of his age, Manrique accepts the division of labor between the Christian who aspires to perfection and the average Christian. But it is more than a little doubtful that he accepts the corresponding evaluation. In any case, he tells us that 'the good monks' gain 'lasting life' by '*prayers and tears*'. By contrast, 'the famous knights' gain it '*by labours and hardships*' in fighting for the faith.

In each of the two cases it is worth noting how the *lay person* conceives and simplifies what would technically be called the active life and the contemplative life. Both come down to sorrow: tears and hardships. The element of mortification is there for both as well, since Manrique writes of prayers and labors. This shows up again in the Ignatian Exercises when the eternal King, describing his own lot, invites the exercitant to "*labor* with me, that by following me in *suffering*, he may follow me in glory" (95).

(4). There is good reason to suspect something here, however, and the verses of Manrique would seem to bear it out. We might suspect that in the medieval historical context, which reached down to Ignatius's own day, the needs, activities, dangers, and adventures of knights, of those engaged in the defense of Christendom especially, had attained such high esteem in the popular mind that the primacy of the contemplative or even religious life was no longer so assured or taken for granted.[93]

Do we not notice something of this different valuation in Manrique's verses, and precisely when he is writing about lasting life:

> . . . the good monks
> gain it by prayers
> and tears;
> the famous knights
> by labours and hardships
> against the Moors.

If we cannot surely detect the slightest note of contempt in the first part of the strophe, it is nevertheless obvious that Manrique shows no special venera-tion for the way in which religious gain eternal life. The vigor of the strophe testifies to that. Manrique writes of 'the famous knights' and seems to put their feats at least on a par with those of religious.

Here, as in the Exercises, we see a groping attempt to link Christian perfec-tion to a project, a project for which God needs human beings: human beings in the world and endowed with traits that can be translated into historical force.

It is not yet the hour, of course, for a christology from below—one which would permit the kingdom of God as proclaimed by the historical Jesus or even the humanization and maturity of humanity espoused by Paul's christology—to take shape in a spirituality. But we do glimpse a return to the more original christology, a project-christology, despite all the tension and inconsistencies we have already noted. Such a christology is one that translates into an active life and stands in need of historical ideologies. In it the ultimate criterion, obscure but certain, is the real-life service one can render to a cause identical with that of Jesus in ever-changing and complicated contexts. Thus, the christology of the Exercises, in its own halting and incipient way, if you will, does give utterance to the deeper needs of its age.

II

It does not solve them, of course. At this point we can only conclude that without a profound transformation of content and method the Ignatian Exer-cises, as they were written and as they are wont to be given today in the footsteps of Ignatius, constitute a spirituality based on a christology that *today* seems incomplete and incorrect, or, at the very least, opposed to clearcut points in the theology of Vatican II and, insofar as Latin America specifically is concerned, the Medellín documents.

This negative judgment is not intended to diminish Ignatius Loyola, but it does say something about the use of the Exercises today. We have seen that the intrinsic difficulties of the Exercises bear witness to a crucial moment in the posing of christological issues in the West, where the Christian context had been shaped by and in the Middle Ages. How was Christianity to move from a christology of test and imitation to a christology centered around a historical project?

That move would open a large breach in the security and certainty felt by the medieval Christian in handling and using christology, and in placing its most profound and demanding version in the service of the contemplative life, a life apart from the world.

That this tentative groping is already in the exercises is demonstrated, I think, by the now classic description of the spirituality issuing from them as 'contemplation *in action*'. That description might well conceal how foolish such an undertaking appeared in Ignatius's own age.

The structure that Ignatius gave to the Society of Jesus excluded those who were seeking 'lasting life' only 'by prayers and tears'. The companions, like 'the famous knights', would gain it 'by labours and hardships against . . . '.

But against whom specifically? Because action was not an end in itself, nor was it supposed to serve merely secondary or superficial ends. It was supposed to be a real, historical, conflict-ridden service for the greater glory of God. The king of the Exercises invites his followers to 'conquer the whole world'.

It is here that the Exercises could not escape their age. Contemplation in action presupposes a *theology of history*, i.e., an understanding of the faith as immersed in the signs of the times, so that it can be contemplated *there*. It needs epistemological premises to discern the presence of God's project in the signs of history.

The general opinion is that the Middle Ages did not provide Christians with the mental tools to ponder history: partly, perhaps, because the period was too dependent on the essentialist philosophy of the Greeks and partly, as well, because it was busy building a stable kind of society on Christian foundations.

What was clear as that period came to a close, and Ignatius evidently was aware of it, was that the old Christian order had suffered a serious split and that new crusades of some sort were needed. This time they might not be aimed so much against those across the frontiers of Christendom as against disruptive factors at work at its very center.

Be that as it may, my concern here is to point up some of the more important elements that made it impossible for the christology of the time to provide properly historical elements of discernment for confronting the new tasks implicit in the Renaissance. Speaking in broad terms, we can say that from the rule of Constantine (when Christianity became an imperial and then imperative religion) to the end of the Middle Ages, everything that went beyond the history of the individual was more or less absolutized and immobilized in two major camps: the friends versus the enemies of the kingdom of God, i.e., *of the Church*.

This mistaken identification of the kingdom of God with the Church as the provider of salvation was not simply the result of the use of power. The temptation in that direction is already evident in the New Testament. But it nevertheless became an inevitable and omnipresent fact when civil authority was exercised in the name of Jesus Christ and associated, rightly or wrongly, with the central term in his own message about the kingdom. The interests of the one and the other seemed to coincide, and to come to rest in something that was mainly to be *preserved* against the twin dangers of internal division (heresies) and external invasion (pagans on the frontiers).

Thus the Church, without ceasing to be immersed in history, emerged from it, thanks to 'eternal' criteria that on the one hand corresponded to a natural law and on the other hand had been revealed to the Church more certainly and explicitly than to the rest of humanity.

Thus we find an undeniably logical sequence between the 'historical' enterprise of the eternal King, who proposes 'to conquer the whole world and all my enemies' (95), and one of the rules to foster 'the true attitude of mind we ought to have in the church militant' (352). The rule is this: "If we wish *to proceed securely in all things*, we must hold fast to the following principle: What seems to me white, I will believe black if the hierarchical Church so defines" (365).

I prescind here from the confusion in this rule because it fails to distinguish between the obligation imposed by faith to accept the *transcendent data* that are part of it and the even more basic obligation to be truthful with respect to the perception of *empirical data*.[94] My interest here is to see where Ignatius turns to find a 'truth' capable of grounding his 'militant' enterprise or project.

Here we come to something subtle and significant. Ignatius will go looking for the criterion of *historical* discernment in that part of the Church which seems to him to retain an atemporal possession of the truth. It is there he will anchor his Society of Jesus, as we shall see a bit more fully in the following pages.

Ignatius will not ask himself if the 'hierarchical' Church is the most sensitive to the signs of the times as they relate to the kingdom of God. The full significance of this is evident when we consider the kingdom as it was preached by Jesus. For his criterion Jesus had an empirical reality as shocking as it was difficult to define in 'eternal' terms: how to make happy the poor and sinners, who were one and the same group. Jesus found historical sensitivity to this criterion precisely in those in Israel who were totally incapable of availing themselves of atemporal and apparently unreformable criteria such as those of the letter of the law.

When Ignatius tries to give permanent orientation to the active service that he and his group plan to offer to the kingdom of God, a particular christology consistent with what we have just seen above will provide him with the answer he wants. It is the substitute or 'vicar' of Christ on earth, who is also the head of the Church, that will indicate to him the 'missions' where their service is especially needed and worthwhile. This explains the fourth vow of obedience to the pope taken by professed Jesuits with respect to 'missions', in the broad sense that this term will assume. Jesuits will enter secret China, try to establish contact with the mysterious and elusive Prester John, and get involved in the political repression of nascent Anglicanism. Whatever the mission may be, all this characterizes Ignatius's idea of the 'action' in the midst of which Jesuits are to *contemplate* in order to render effective service by imitating Jesus.[95]

Obviously, the room left for freedom in such unforeseen enterprises is much wider than that fixed by the established Christian order. The means are relativized,[96] and that forces Ignatius to look more and more outside the Exercises for the criteria behind the corresponding discernment. A whole new world, unforeseen and unexplored, will gradually open up before the 'missions' that are to be undertaken.

This is also intimately bound up with the explosion of the 'Christian' West. In the Renaissance the perceptible cohesion between *faith* and *ideology* is lost. The values of Jesus begin to take unexpected pathways, sometimes apart from, and sometimes opposed to, those *officially* regarded as such. What Vatican II will later state boldly begins to be a plausible hypothesis: i.e., that the genesis of atheism is partly or sometimes due to the fact that people espouse certain values in the name of the Christian God when those values are, in fact, opposed to Christian values and the Christian God; hence the rejection of those antivalues is more deeply Christian than their acceptance or espousal.

The autonomous development of science and the explosion of a more or less homogeneous faith into the world will produce systems of efficacy whose independent life will become increasingly perceptible as time goes on. Insofar as it tries to retain its purity and validity by mere adherence to certain dogmas, the Christian faith will become increasingly isolated from the systems of efficacy that arise outside it under the aegis of one or another form of humanism. Thus, *efficacy* in the service of the faith will become increasingly uncritical of the meaning and implications of the concrete struggle, which will be exacerbated by the return to the *ancien régime* and Christendom, or their partial preservation.

The christology of the Ignatian Exercises is a first step in the conversion of a static test-christology into a dynamic project-christology. But it is still too dominated by elements 'from above', and hence its interpretation of Jesus clearly lacks the criteria needed to imagine the pathways opening up to the kingdom of God and its progress in the secular world that is beginning to take shape.

APPENDIX

A Christology Encounters History

Perhaps my readers may be interested if I proceed a bit further with my study of the tentative christology surfacing in Ignatius's thought and work. I do so precisely because his historical context posed a new challenge in the West: i.e., the complexity of *secular history*. It was not simply a matter of shifting from a test-christology to a project-christology. It would become increasingly clear that the problem in the interpretation of Jesus of Nazareth was to find criteria for judging projects that were not directly identifiable with 'the greater glory of God'.

We must not forget that the case of Ignatius is merely one example among countless others that might be even more relevant. Nor must we forget that the effort under study here could not be carried through to completion in Ignatius's own time. We are looking at groping efforts that are meaningful, especially, I would say, for those who have followed me this far in my analysis of the christological elements in the Ignatian Exercises.

One important fact should be kept in mind. We are shifting our focus from the early personal experiences of Ignatius, to which the Exercises correspond, to certain relevant characteristics of his later activity as founder, legislator, and superior of a new religious order, the Society of Jesus. For it is there, logically enough, that he will be forced to confront the historical complexity of his age, not from Spain any longer but from the very center of dissolving Western Christendom: Rome.

We already know that the Exercises themselves related to two well-defined periods in Ignatius's life: the time of his own personal experiences in Manresa, and the time of his formal theological study in Paris. Both of those periods preceded his establishment of the Society of Jesus and the two essential tasks it entailed for him: providing the order with basic legislation and concretely directing its activities.

It also seems obvious that after his Paris studies, especially with the inauguration of the Society of Jesus in quick order, Ignatius did not become familiar with another christology or take any great interest in theological problems. For

115

a while he continued to direct the Spiritual Exercises; later he would focus on giving guidance to others who were directing them. There seems to be no doubt that Ignatius never *explicitly saw* anything in the Exercises or that activity that clashed with his understanding of God, Christ, and the Church as he experienced those realities vis-à-vis his own life and that of his religious order.

Does that mean that nothing changed in his spirituality? To take a specific date, by way of example: Does that mean that Ignatius as superior general of the Jesuits in 1553, thirty years after his experiences in Manresa and twenty years after his work on the Paris portion of the Exercises, was still thinking and acting in accordance with *the christology* he put in the Exercises and its derivative theological and practical lines contained in the Exercises? As far as I know, all the historians of the subject answer 'yes' to those questions; and 'yes' would seem to be the required answer of all those who claim that the 'charism' of the Society of Jesus lies in its 'spirituality', the latter being found in the Ignatian Exercises.

My answer is 'no', and it is the basic hypothesis I defend in this Appendix. I have already dealt with the hesitant turn of the Exercises from a test-christology toward a project-christology. I now maintain that the impossibility of fully structuring the latter christology in the Exercises led Ignatius to move away from certain categories peculiar to the Exercises as he became increasingly involved in making historical decisions.

The transformation is subtle and implicit, to be sure, so it can always be denied by those who stick to the explicit, direct statements of the documentary evidence. But I maintain that such a transformation does indeed take place, contributing a paradoxical but definitely positive quality to Ignatius's christology.

I

There are relatively clear signs of this transformation. The first, which I would call inevitable, is the complete *historicization* of the term 'service' in Ignatius's correspondence, as opposed to its ambiguous usage in the Exercises. As we move away in time from the Exercises, the term 'service' connotes something increasingly different from 'praising and reverencing'. While the latter two terms remain ahistorical, the term 'service' comes to mean turning into reality, within the course of actual events, a 'will of God' that one has to 'feel' or 'perceive'. We could almost say 'smell', since it is a difficult thing for which there are no preestablished criteria and one must pray continually to hit upon it.

The same holds true for 'glory' and other similar terms, but it is far more noticeable with respect to 'service' and its surrounding conditions. Ignatius now discards the view that 'service' means fulfillment of the law and that 'greater service' has to do with a more complete imitation of Jesus in his passion. Service now implies the strategy to make the cause of God and Christ triumphant in history. It is no longer a *means*, as it was in the First Principle and Foundation, nor does it even come down to 'distinguishing oneself more' by choosing a more total imitation. To be sure, the 'more' (*magis*) so characteristic of the Exercises never disappears from the spirituality of Ignatius. But it is impossible not to notice the shift from the subjective to the objective, from the interior life to the realm of history.

So we see that the imitation of Christ, i.e., a christology designed to complement the test-theology with *the supreme example* of God's preferences, does not seem to count for much in the decisions Ignatius makes about the members of his 'Company'. By way of example, here is his reply to Manuel Godinho, who was involved in temporal administration and undoubtedly concerned about the criterion of imitation given in the Exercises: "With respect to the management of temporal things, though it may somehow seem and be distracting, I have no doubt that your holy intention and your *dedication of all you do to God's glory* will make it spiritual and very pleasing to his infinite goodness. For distractions accepted for *his greater service* and in conformity with his divine will, as interpreted through obedience, can be not only equivalent but *even more acceptable.* . . . The double spirit you say is necessary, may it be given to you in abundance by He who gave it to Elijah. . . . "[97]

Here is another datum. We no longer see the third kind of humility showing up as a criterion of choice once people become members of the Society of Jesus. Although likeness to Christ poor, insulted, and regarded as a fool may give inspiration and consolation to those who find themselves in that situation through no fault of their own, the greater service of God calls for immersion in the processes of secular history, an immersion that is deeper, more respectful of the relative, and therefore efficacious. This explains the 'worldly' and almost economical prudence of the advice Ignatius gives to Charles V of Spain to put an end to the naval incursions of the Turks in the Mediterranean.[98]

Much the same happens to the 'indifference' called for in the First Principle and Foundation. In the Exercises, Ignatius seems to move from criterion to criterion trying to find out where it may finally become a decided *preference* for something. Indifference does not disappear as we move away from the Exercises, but now *preference* precedes it and makes it meaningful. It becomes increasingly synonymous with making oneself 'available' and flexible because projects call for changes, switches from accustomed means to unfamiliar ones, and sensitivity to changes in historical situations and their accompanying logical implications. This transformation may seem subtle, but it is certainly radical.

Perhaps there is no clearer example of this shift in the meaning of 'indifference' than Ignatius's attitude and approach to the pope. In the abstract, that attitude and approach still seem much like indifference, as when he writes to Bobadilla: "Given that our profession is to *offer our persons* so that we may be sent wherever the vicar of our Lord Jesus Christ finds it advisable, and as seems best to him, . . . I, judging it was licit for me, in speaking to others, to point out or *hint at* your needs there, so that in providing or not providing they would do what seemed *more to the glory of God our Lord*, in accordance with what you wrote me, I spoke with Cardinal Santa Cruz and Cardinal Morón. With that *I would be very content*, being there and accepting what is necessary from whatever hand you felt came from God Our Lord. . . . "[99]

But what are we to say of Ignatius's 'indifference' prior to the decisions that were finally reached about his 'Company' by the 'Theatine' Cardinal Caraffa once he had been elevated to the papal throne as Paul IV? Is it anything more than *availability* and that after having moved heaven and earth to tip the scale to one side? Yet the Exercises tell us that the 'indifferent' person "should be like a balance at equilibrium, without leaning to either side" (179).

An even more significant indication of this transformation is the almost scandalous letter that Ignatius wrote to Le Jay, Salmerón, and Canisius in Ingolstadt to inform them of the election of the new pope: "First, that Del Monte is pope, who made them doctors. Second, that the cardinals who *can do most* with him are Burgos, Carpi, the Theatine, Santa Cruz, and Mafeo, in that order."[100] Such things have been taken as indications that Ignatius had an enormous will to power. I disagree. I think that they, like the data noted above, point to an increasingly determined involvement in historical causality.

To some extent I think we can say that this letter reveals the distance in time separating Ignatius's effort in the Exercises to find signs from heaven about the will of God from his later effort to make openings for the projects of Christ through the signs of the times.

The ultimate criterion of discernment, which raised so much debate in the Exercises because of its elusive character, now consciously occupies first place: " . . . provided, of course, that it be for the service and praise of the Divine Goodness" (157). But the aura of mystery surrounding it has disappeared.

It is no longer necessary, it seems, to have recourse to almost miraculous interventions of the Creator acting directly on the creature in order to establish it. Throughout Ignatius's correspondence we find what I would call a process of demythologization. Some might argue that his letters are not the mystical work that the Exercises are. But all the more significant, then, is Ignatius's reaction when some Jesuits, Oviedo for example, dare to allude to direct communications from God in prayer: "Here one has a hard time understanding this new genre of *miracles*. . . . The term 'miracle' is attributed to a few *rare* works of God outside the ordinary course instituted by his divine wisdom. . . ."[101]

Though it is not easy to spell out the exact meaning of that response, its tendency and intent is obviously in the direction of 'demythologizing'. It is also worth noting that in it direct communication with God —which is normally assumed in the Exercises[102]—does not provide a sufficient and reliable criterion. It must be subject to another criterion that seems to be earthly and profane, and above all, historical: "The third reason is that when God our Lord reveals *supernatural things of that sort, he is wont [!] to do it for some good end, seeking something useful to human beings,* . . . but . . . we find no usefulness, . . . rather, harm and scandal for those in the Society, if they believe them, and for those outside."[103]

But it may well be by examining the arguments opposed to my hypotheses that it will be established as fully plausible, if not definitively proved.

II

Two arguments militate against my hypothesis. The first is that we must not confuse the Ignatian spirituality that precedes and accompanies the choice of a way of life (i.e., the spirituality of the Exercises) with that which follows the choice and is embodied in such things as Ignatius's correspondence as superior general of the Society of Jesus. The second argument is that, despite the apparent direction of the previous argument, we have sufficient data to maintain that Ignatius always remained faithful to the very same spiritual methods and criteria that brought him such results in Manresa.

The conclusion resulting from these two arguments against my hypothesis would come down to this: if there is any change, it does not signify or entail a transformation in the first or early spirituality of Ignatius; it merely signifies a difference in contexts. And not even that, of course, if in fact there is no change.

The *first argument* is a serious one, and it is not without historical indications that lend support to it. People have too readily and naturally taken it for granted that the Ignatian Exercises constitute an ongoing 'spirituality' coextensive with the Christian life. The fact is that they are a methodology for an intensive month during which the exercitants immerse themselves in the truths of faith in order to choose their course in life. In other words, we may have lost sight of the fact that the Exercises are *a means situated in a specific context: i.e., choosing a way of life.*

The Ignatius who went through the experiences of Manresa and recorded the results in the Exercises was a Christian in search of his vocation. Thus, there is a fundamental difference between the Exercises of Ignatius on the one hand and the *Interior Castle* of Teresa or the *Ascent of Mount Carmel* of John of the Cross on the other. The latter two works are long, complete itineraries of the soul. That difference may not be perceived clearly enough by those who simply want to endow the Society of Jesus with a 'spirituality' in the broadest sense and resort to the Exercises for this purpose.

The Exercises are very clear about their limited purpose, if you will, which is 'seeking and finding the will of God *in the disposition* of our life' (1), or 'the regulation of one's life' (21). Both of these converge in the *choice of a way of life*, or at least some form of choice 'for the amendment and reformation of one's way of living in his state of life' (189).

Aside from some general rules equally valid for other occasions, everything in the Exercises seems to be a strategy for *choosing* the general orientation of one's life *in accordance with the will of God*. It is more than doubtful that Ignatius thought of them as a permanent, much less annual, form of spiritual retreat.[104]

Now the first argument against my hypothesis stresses that this point where all the Exercises converge, i.e., the choice of a way of life or the reform of one's life, has already passed when we come to the correspondence of Ignatius. This explains all the differences, it maintains, and those differences do not signify any fundamental change. The fundamental choice has been made. Now a Christian confronts a path that has been traced out, with its problems and vicissitudes. The more practical and concrete criteria to go by on this journey are of a different order and are to be established in a different way. The 'spirituality' of this new Ignatius is to be sought more in his thinking about the life and activity of the members of his Society than in the Exercises directly.

This argument deserves consideration, all the more insofar as it is fairly similar to my own hypothesis in some respects. Its flaw, I think, lies in its attempt to explain the change within an overall unity. For all its *historical* continuity with Ignatius's choice of a way of life, what follows afterwards presupposes new and *different* criteria for deciding important matters, in my opinion. Those criteria, in turn, imply or entail a definite *theological* discontinuity. My hypothesis, in other words, is that we are dealing here not merely with a shift to a more practical or concrete theology but with a *distinct* theology and its corresponding christology, which could not achieve its full coherence and express its originality with the available theological elements of the time. I am claiming that the Society of Jesus represents the fruit of a different theological view of how to serve Jesus and the kingdom, one that in important points is far removed from that which dominates the Exercises.

Consider just this one thing, for example. *Nothing* in the Exercises points to following Jesus precisely or necessarily in the religious order that Ignatius will found. If the Exercises could be isolated from other psychosocial variables—who gives them, where they take place, how exercitants are recruited—they would produce vocations indiscriminately for any and every religious order. In fact, however, Ignatius probably made the Exercises as we do today and did not decide to enter any existing religious order. It is impossible for us to say exactly why. All we can see is that he was looking for something else, in the light of the Exercises and the 'choice' he made in them, without clearly perceiving what.

We know that later Ignatius did think about entering a religious order. He did not decide to do so, even though he found inspiration and consolation in the thought.[105] Am I mistaken or off base in thinking that this hesitancy and oscillation were due in some measure to the loose threads left in the Exercises, threads we now know to be closely bound up with theological and christological elements?

My simple hypothesis is that it was only as Ignatius gathered 'companions' around him and founded the 'Company of Jesus' that he gradually found the elements which he still needed and which were not in the Exercises; but those elements always remained implicit, and he never gave them theological shape or form.[106] So his most profound christology, be it good or bad, must be sought much more in the structure and orientation he gave to his religious order than in the Exercises; and to find that, we must look at his correspondence.

The *second argument* against my hypothesis is the favorite one of historians, as we might logically guess. Here is one example: "His letters . . . are a commentary on the Exercises, as it were . . . the very same ideas, the very same principles. The difference is in the concrete way of projecting the very same truths. In his letters they are reflected from a more practical point of view, in terms of their concrete, real-life applications. That helps us to probe more deeply into aspects that are in danger of being overlooked in the Exercises, or at least not so easily noticed."[107]

There would really be no point in examining the actual material behind such statements, which could always be proved from the literal text. The shadings I allude to in the first section of this Appendix can only be analyzed with instruments of a different preciseness, at least in their theological aspect.

Let me take an example related to an essential point of the Exercises: *making a choice*. The pope wanted to give the cardinal's hat to Francis Borgia, the duke of Gandia, who had been admitted to the Society of Jesus in 1546. Faced with this situation, Ignatius had to make a 'choice'. From his correspondence we know that in 1552, when all this was going on, Ignatius was still using the 'second time' of making a choice indicated in the Exercises, "When much light and understanding are derived through experience of desolations and consolations and discernment of diverse spirits"(176).

In one of his letters to Borgia that year, Ignatius describes his own feelings and his way of proceeding in some detail. He was not sure of God's will because he was getting reasons in support of two different views. He gave house orders for priests to say Mass and lay members to offer up prayers for three days that everything might be governed by what would lead 'to the greater glory of God'. During the three days, Ignatius sometimes felt certain fears as he contemplated the matter: " . . . not the freedom of spirit to discuss or stand in the way of the matter. I said to myself: what do I know about what God our Lord wants to do? I did not feel entirely sure about standing in the way. At other times, in my usual periods of prayer, I felt those fears disappearing. . . . Finally, on the third day, I found myself praying as usual, and then with such complete judgment and such a gentle and free will to stand in the way, which was in my mind, before the pope and the cardinals, that if I had not done that, I would have felt and do feel for certain that I could not give a good account of myself to God, quite the contrary."[108]

This is not the only testimony, or the main testimony, to Ignatius's fidelity to this precise point in the Exercises. Thus, the argument for continuity is *literally* indestructible. But we have every right to ask the following questions about the method that he continues to use: Does it occupy the same *theological place*? Does it fulfill the same function?

In the Exercises, as we saw, this 'time' of making a choice practically occupies the central place. It is the surest criterion—aside from the relatively rare 'first time'. It is through this approach more than any other that a person is to seek the elusive definitive criterion for the most important of all personal affairs: the disposition of one's *whole life*.

In the Borgia case, however, we notice several theologically significant characteristics that point in a different direction. The case was important, to be sure, and it was with good reason that Ignatius dedicated three days of reflection, prayer, and conversation to it in a life that was relatively intense already. But that very same importance seems to be reduced insofar as the principal criterion is concerned. The fact is that Ignatius saw many reasons on both sides of the issue, as we learn from his letter. His bold Spanish makes clear how he saw the problem as a whole: "What do I know about what God our Lord wants to do?" An exclamation point might seem more appropriate than a question mark at the end of that statement, even though it is framed as a question.

The various reasons for and against the cardinal's hat for Borgia persuaded Ignatius that either course might serve the glory and praise of God. Some were for it, some were against it; the same divine spirit might be behind both feelings, prompting him to take one side while other people took the opposite view.[109] This makes all the more interesting the theological basis that led Ignatius to adopt the attitude or approach, in his dealings with the pope and the cardinals, that he picturesquely describes as 'standing in the way'. And that is so not just of the theological basis of his attitude or position but also of the theological basis of the method he chooses in order to arrive at it.

I would remind readers of Ignatius's written remark to Faber. He tells Faber that in some brief period of time, not specified exactly ('now'), he had written about two hundred and fifty letters, and that this was more or less a regular, ongoing obligation he faced.[110] So the *reason* for using the 'second time' of choice for three days in the Borgia case must have had something to do with a *theological place*, i.e., with a particular characteristic of the problem in question.

In the many other cases he resolved daily, we must assume that the *simplicity of the elements involved*, not the lesser importance of the issue to be resolved, was what enabled him to make a quick 'choice' or decision. In the Borgia case, by contrast, it is not its crucial importance but its historical complexity that forces him to seek the criterion for making a choice in a different way. In other words, the historical context has assumed a new *theological place* in something that, on the surface, might seem to be a mere continuation of the methods for choosing that are found in the Exercises.

Precisely the same considerations hold true for a very special case. We possess only a small part of Ignatius's *Spiritual Diary*, but from it we learn that Ignatius used the same method as in the Borgia case, and for a whole month, to resolve the matter of the poverty of the churches belonging to the 'professed houses' of his order, which could not have revenues. Iparraguirre, moreover, tells us that Ignatius's *Spiritual Diary* is really 'nothing more than the Exercises in action'.[111] Father Iparraguirre adds that Ignatius proceeded the same way in drawing up all the Constitutions of the Society of Jesus.[112]

From the theological standpoint, which is the one that interests us here, I must point out two things that are quite clear. First, if we consider merely the *quantity* of topics, not to mention their importance, that enter the Constitutions, the simplest arithmetic calculation will tell us that Ignatius could not have used the method to resolve all the matters in the Constitutions. If he had used that time-consuming method to resolve every question, only a minimum amount of the Constitutions could have been written before the founder's death. Second, even if we grant that Ignatius presented the constitutional point under consideration to God at his daily Mass, that does not mean he used the 'second time' of choice for all of them, or even for the most important ones. Ignatius's choice in these matters undoubtedly followed a less mystical and more 'historical' path, if you will allow me the word.

Father Iparraguirre, editor of the *Obras completas* from which I cite in this volume, offers this comment on a letter of Ignatius to Laínez: "Almost as soon as he was elected superior general of the Society, St. Ignatius had to begin thinking about legislation for his order. Since it was a matter of the *utmost importance*, he preferred to proceed gradually. Before establishing definitive norms, *he was trying them out and observing* the difficulties arising from their practice."[113] This particular letter of Ignatius to Laínez, bidding him to try out certain norms, is dated a year prior to the deliberations noted in what we have of his *Spiritual Diary*.

We may logically ask ourselves, therefore: What special characteristics did the concrete issue of the poverty of the churches attached to professed houses possess that many other matters in the Constitutions did not possess? If Ignatius customarily used another method of choosing or deciding on other matters, a method we might call one of 'historical verification', why did he depart from that approach with regard to this concrete issue?

We would undoubtedly be led astray if we tried to relate this question to the relative importance of the issues. At first glance we could say that the cardinal's hat was important for Borgia, whereas deciding whether the churches could or could not have their own income, even though the houses had to live off alms, was a small matter. But the proof that Ignatius deems both important is the time he devotes to solving the problems they pose in the midst of his overburdened life.

A more likely hypothesis is that it is not so much the *crucial* nature of these issues that determines Ignatius's specific mode of choosing, a mode that differentiates them from other issues. Rather, it is the *complexity* of the reasons that makes it difficult for him to see clearly what is truly consistent with the general project he is trying to carry out. In the case under discussion here, in fact, the 'companions' had already decided that the poverty of their professed houses was not violated by the fact that their churches accepted revenues allocated exclusively to the necessities of divine worship.[114]

With respect to the second argument against my hypothesis, I do not get the impression that the Ignatius who had to resolve problems and fashion the structure of the Society of Jesus was a person in permanent Spiritual Exercises, so to speak. Rather, it seems that history—with its relativity, its experimentation, and its efficacy tied to a consistent quest for the same objective in different places and times—was progressively becoming the most important and common theological place to which Ignatius had recourse in the last phase of his life.

To repeat once again: the difference may seem subtle, but I think it is theologically worthy of consideration. The order of the criteria presented by the Exercises had been changed. And it is not so much the success of the change as the necessity of it that attracts our attention.

•

To sum up: my impression is that as we move farther away from the epoch of the Exercises in the life of Ignatius Loyola, we find that the criteria for choosing that are given in the Exercises no longer govern the historical interpretaion demanded by his task vis-à-vis the Society of Jesus.

Ignatius now hears Jesus speaking to him from a place he had disregarded earlier: from the very history he was obliged to live; and in a world to be changed, the importance of which was being revealed to him more and more. Or, to put it more accurately, Ignatius tries to hear Jesus speaking to him from within history even when his theology fails to provide him with the mediations needed to decipher that historical key. It is precisely when and insofar as he somehow perceives those deficiencies in some cases, when he feels disconcerted by his own ignorance or uncertainty ('What do I know . . . ?'), that he falls back on the more atemporal modes of choosing he had cultivated in the first phase, which was now surpassed. If he himself did not remind us constantly in his letters that the matter at hand was the kingdom of God, the project of Christ, we could almost say that the 'demon' of *history* had taken possession of him.

It is obviously up to my readers to form their own judgment on this whole matter, insofar as they have an interest in it. It was not the aim of this volume to pass final judgment on the *Spiritual Exercises* of Ignatius Loyola. My aim was to point out, in a living example rather than in merely abstract terms, the vicissitudes of a christology. On the one hand, that christology had lost one of its dimensions, and hence its historical flexibility. On the other hand, under the stimulus of a significant change in the surrounding historical context, it perceived its original creative vocation: to interpret Jesus of Nazareth anew in terms of the challenges of a Renaissance world that the New Testament itself could not have imagined.

Thus, my aim has simply been to show my readers one link in the christological chain that reaches down to us and again places us before the same challenge.

Notes

Introduction: Christologies in Christian Spiritualities

1. See Chapter I in this volume.
2. J. Manrique, "Verses on the Death of his Father," in *The Penguin Book of Spanish Verse,* pp. 40–59. See entry under Manrique in the Reference Bibliography.
3. Manrique, pp. 57–58. Segundo italics throughout.
4. Ibid., p. 58.
5. Ibid., p. 59.
6. Ibid.
7. Although I am not a historian and hence cannot be fully certain of it, I think it would be useless to go looking *directly* in the more or less academic theology of Manrique's age for traces of the view that the sureness of salvation is in direct proportion to the amount of pagan blood spilled. It may be a case of literary exaggeration, after all. It is the poet's way of saying that Manrique the Knight clearly took seriously the defense of the faith, performing that task in what was regarded as the best possible way in his day. The relationship between the poet's statement and theology is much more subtle, in all likelihood. It probably lies in some sort of identification between the universality of the Church and the establishment of the kingdom of God. The important point for us here is that in such texts the cultural certitudes about religion are expressed openly and naïvely, without much concern about how well they dovetail with classroom theology.
8. Some readers may be disgusted with my use of the term 'spirituality' to designate the various conceptions of the faith that were actually and explicitly lived out on a day-to-day basis within Christianity. Even so, any and every history of Christianity, from at least the Middle Ages to today, must devote whole chapters to those *schools* of Christian living that arose over the centuries and vied with each other for first place. The pejorative connotation that the term 'spirituality' has taken on, at least in some circles, stems from the theoretical and practical opposition that existed in theology—and passed over into life—between two planes or levels of reality, one of which was called precisely the 'spiritual' or 'supernatural' level. On this higher plane people discussed 'supernatural' or 'eternal' problems about redemption and the salvation of the soul. The lower plane or level was the 'temporal' plane, which was considered 'purely natural'. It had to do with the order of creation, which

125

was destined to disappear with the end of history. This scheme of two separate planes collapsed when more recent theology, backed up by major passages of Vatican II and *Gaudium et spes* in particular, destroyed in theory the underlying principle of any such separation, pointing out that the faith "throws a new light on everything, manifests God's design for humanity's total vocation, and thus directs the mind to fully human solutions" of historical problems (GS:11). With this collapse of the two separate planes, the terms 'spiritual' and 'spirituality' were unfairly given overtones of being preconciliar, of suggesting a brand of Christianity lived in despite of history. But liberation theologians themselves, for example, are now pleading for the creation of a suitable liberation 'spirituality', i.e., a way to flesh out in life what they accept in theory. See, for example: G. Gutiérrez, *A Theology of Liberation,* Chapter Ten, p. 203 f.; idem, *We Drink from Our Own Wells*; S. Galilea, "Liberation Theology and New Tasks Facing Christians," final section on the approach to a liberation spirituality; Donal Dorr, *Spirituality and Justice.*

9. Reinhold Niebuhr, *The Nature and Destiny of Man,* II, 92–93.

10. Ibid.

11. Ibid., p. 93.

12. Ibid., p. 92. Similar observations might be made about the spirituality of the *Imitatio Christi,* especially as we find it in the widely known and used work of Thomas à Kempis by that name. See my comments in J. L. Segundo, *Grace and the Human Condition,* p. 87 f.

13. The clearest example known to me is the Appendix that Jon Sobrino devotes to "The Christ of the Ignatian Exercises" in his *Christology at the Crossroads,* pp. 396–424.

Chapter I: Jesus and God: Approach to the Council of Chalcedon

14. Readers will find a fuller and well-presented version of this review in Christian Duquoc, *Cristología,* Chapter VII. Section II of that chapter deals with the ecclesial interpretation of Christ's sonship up to the Council of Chalcedon. Section III deals with the personal oneness of Christ. See ibid., pp. 250–72.

15. As I explained in Volume III, I chose only one of those christologies, that of Paul in Romans 1–8, to point up the creative process whereby Paul moved from the historical data on Jesus to an interpretation of the meaningful change his history and paschal experiences introduced into human existence. Obviously my methodological intention would have been even better grounded and proved if I had repeated the same process with the many other christologies in the New Testament: that of each of the Synoptic writers, of John, of the Letter to the Hebrews, and so forth.

16. Gregory Bateson, "Why a Swan?" in *Steps to an Ecology of Mind,* pp. 33–37.

17. Indeed in any of the prophets or writers of the Old Testament there is a shift to still *another* higher logical level, which does not even have to do with

what *Jeremiah says that Yahweh indicates* about how to differentiate a true prophecy from a false prophecy. This other level is the one that made it possible historically to accept Jeremiah, and not his rival for example, as part of the book or books (*biblia* is a plural) containing Yahweh's revelation, that tradition of learning to learn which, if it is to exist at all, must begin by rejecting as irrelevant or false many other claims of receiving revelations from Yahweh that were made by historical personages in Israel.

18. It seems certain that during the Galilean crisis Jesus did ask about the relationship to God that the multitude and then his own disciples attributed to him; but this was done within the narrow circle of his own disciples. In those very specific circumstances he does not seem to have rejected the identification of himself with the Messiah. But that instance and, even more, his declaration of Messiahship before the Sandhedrin were restricted to a very limited audience and inspired by a very special set of circumstances. Even in those instances, priority is given to the proximity of the kingdom. Moreover, in his public life it is the kingdom that always shows up as central. Its slowness in arriving, we might also note, is what probably provoked his anguished cry on the cross. He felt that there had been some sort of mistake in his calculus, which surely was grounded on his relationship with the deity.

19. When I say the Canticle of Canticles is a 'unique case', I am referring only to the clarity with which it poses our problem. It is not unique in terms of its essential features, even in the Old Testament. In this connection Gerhard von Rad makes some relevant observations about the history of Solomon's succession to the throne of David, his father. See Von Rad, "Los comienzos de la historiografía en el antiguo Israel," in *Estudios sobre el Antiguo Testamento,* p. 141 f.

20. See, for example, Is 5:7. Von Rad (ibid., p. 171 f.) points out how the biblical authors proceeded, several centuries before the Canticle of Canticles, to unite apparently profane events with the revelation of a divine project or evaluation. That approach is entirely lacking here. It is not that the habit of using it had been lost, as the Book of Proverbs and, later, the Book of Sirach will show. In those books the mention of God is used, in most passages where it occurs, only to *elevate* to the level of the sacred a profane wisdom that has been acquired by human experience and that is often characterized by a surprising, almost cynical pragmatism.

21. Those who might object that this blessing was withdrawn because of Adam's original sin would have to be reminded that the blessing was withdrawn from marriage specifically (see Gen 3:16 f.).

22. See Werner Jaeger, *Paideia: The Ideals of Greek Culture.*

23. Note that I refer to the divine aspect of demigods or incarnate gods as a 'contribution' only to the extent that its intervention does not diminish the *human* significance of the personage. For then we get a situation such as that which occurred with Greek education (and with other parallel cases): i.e., that anthropological faith will depend more on the human beings than on the gods. One of the probable causes of the victory of the Judeo-Christian religion over

Greco-Roman religions was its 'pre-Chalcedon' character: i.e., the rejection of divine-human intermixtures in the great biblical figures. The relationship with the divine that was had by such figures as Abraham, Moses, David, Elijah, Jeremiah, and Jesus of Nazareth did not *mix* with their lives in such a way as to strip away the profoundly tragic and human aspects of those lives that were revelatory of God.

24. Soon there also appear, not only titles or isolated phrases referring to the relationship between Jesus and God, but also probable hymns or at least entire poetic passages on the theme. The principal ones are Phil 2:6–11, Col 1:15–20, Eph 1:3–14, Jn 1:1–18, and perhaps certain fragments such as 1 Tm 3:16, 6:15–16, etc.

25. As I noted in Volume III (Chapter V, Section II), Paul has this strain also, despite the overall balance of his treatment. We are so used to this mutilation of the *historical* testimony of Jesus that we do not even blink when we read that "Christ died for us" (Rom 5:8; see 5:6; 4:25; 13:25; etc.). Yet we know well history tells us that he was assassinated by his religious-political adversaries, and that his last words on the cross were: "My God, my God, why have you forsaken me?" (Mk 15:34; Mt 27:46). Commenting on Rom 4:25 ("who had been handed over for our misdeeds . . . "), Duquoc aptly writes: "The whole difficulty with the theology of the cross derives from the obscurity of the connection between the documented fact and the proclamation of the apostolic faith, 'He died for our sins'. The theologies of redemption have tried to clarify this connection. The individual occurrence of a human death, in those theologies, takes on the quality of a universally important event. Unfortunately, those theologies often tear the documented fact out of its specific context and clarify it on the basis of theological concepts, occasionally giving them a historical form" (Duquoc, *Cristología*, p. 368).

26. It is never formulated thus, of course. That would be practically impossible because the Greek of the New Testament documents obliges us right at the start to make a distinction. Depending on whether or not the definite article is used, we must notice whether the predicate attributed to Jesus is *ho theos* (*the* God, Yahweh, the Father, etc.) or *theos* (God, divinity, divine, etc.). In the following pages I shall briefly examine what class or degree of divinity is attributed to Jesus in the New Testament. The point I want to bring out here is a linguistic distinction that is no longer perceptible in our vernacular languages today, where the common noun 'god' has become the proper name 'God', i.e., an essentially unique reality.

27. G. J. Botterweck, *Gott erkennen,* p. 97; cited by José Míguez Bonino in *Christians and Marxists,* pp. 34–35. Unfortunately, Míguez's book came into my hands only after I had written Volume I of the present series. His extraordinary clarity, informativeness, and sound judgment would have spared me much searching, and my readers much of the obscurity they will find here. It seems to me that there is a basic convergence between his work and mine in their general formulation of the issues. If that is not the case, I hope Míguez will pardon my saying so.

28. Míguez Bonino, *Christians and Marxists,* p. 35.

29. Ibid., p. 32.

30. Perhaps we might except the third assertion of the first verse of the Prologue of the fourth Gospel: ' . . . and the Word was God'. But the identification of that Word with Jesus of Nazareth in verse 14 ('we have seen his glory') is done in accordance with the indicated biblical procedure, i.e., in the opposite direction. In other words, it follows the order indicated in the earlier references to 1 John. The result is the divine *glory* is perceived in Jesus in those things that least display divine characteristics *in themselves:* i.e., in his washing of the disciples' feet and in his crucifixion (see Jn 13:1.31–32; 17:1).

31. That such a language exists cannot be doubted, as we shall have occasion to see in the following section on the christological controversies. My point here, however, is that this is not the language used by the Bible. In line with what we have just seen, Míguez Bonino rightly insists: "God does not want to be known—or rather, he will not let himself be known—outside this covenantal relationship: he discloses his 'name', he makes himself known by fulfilling his promises and judgments. This is the meaning of the well-known formula: 'When it happens, then *you will know*'. The relationships that man fancies and fashions with his 'gods' are empty of reality and power; the true God fashions himself a relationship and can only be known within it. There is no neutral, objective, unengaged knowledge of God" (Míguez Bonino, *Christians and Marxists,* p. 107).

32. I say 'seemed' because any meaning given to the word 'love', when applied to the pure act of Aristotelian philosophy, for example, becomes contradictory. The mere fact that God loves by 'creating' a world already contradicts the divine simplicity. The *contingency* of the world, and hence God's freedom to create it, presupposes a distinction between the essence of God and God's will to create, thereby destroying the divine simplicity. Schubert M. Ogden (*The Reality of God,* p. 17) correctly notes: "This is evident, for example, from traditional theological discussions of the creation of the world. Theologians usually tell us that God creates the world freely, as the contingent or nonnecessary world our experience discloses it to be. This assertion is also made necessary because it offers the only really credible construction of the account of creation in Holy Scripture. At the same time, because of their fixed commitment to the assumptions of classical metaphysics, theologians also tell us that God's act of creation is one with his own eternal essence, which is in every respect necessary, exclusive of all contingency. Hence, if we take them at their own word, giving full weight to both of their assertions, we at once find ourselves in the hopeless contradiction of a wholly necessary creation of a wholly contingent world."

33. To the extent that this is true throughout the Bible, I insist that the language under analysis here is not so much rejecting atheism as any and every type of 'religion' that resorts to the seeming 'objectivity' of the religious in order to dehumanize human beings. It was not Marx who discovered that religion could be the opiate of the people. But I must say that in certain periods

of his life Marx was strangely 'idealist' in his 'essential' criticism of religion. To start from the other end, and say it right out: the Bible is not aiming its guns at atheism but at idolatry, and particularly at idolatry garbed in the raiments of formal orthodoxy.

34. The more exact translation of the original Hebrew would be: "You will not permit your *friend* (or, *faithful one*) to experience corruption." Peter cites the text in accordance with the Greek translation of the Septuagint. This linguistic fact is important. In biblical language 'holiness' and 'holy' are equivalent to 'divinity' and 'divine'. A faithful friend of God, who to some extent has ties of friendship with the Absolute, can only be called 'holy', i.e., 'divine', if belonging in an intimate way to the sphere of the Absolute.

35. That is how Pannenberg proceeds in *Jesus—God and Man* (p. 53 f.). The first part of his work deals with 'The Knowledge of Jesus' Divinity' (p. 51). It begins with Chapter III: 'Jesus' Resurrection as the Ground of His Unity with God'. The first part of that chapter considers the prepaschal Jesus: 'The Proleptic Element in Jesus' Claim to Authority'.

36. Most clearly in John's Gospel, not only in the Prologue but elsewhere in statements attributed to Jesus: from the 'I am' (without a complement), which is the biblical way Yahweh names himself, to such statements as 'I am the way, the truth, and the life'.

37. "The criticism of the 'gods' of Greek mythology which these philosophers had undertaken, had issued in a 'purified' idea of 'the essence of god', a 'deity' prior and superior to the anthropomorphic gods of their pantheon. Such an essence could be known through philosophical speculation. . . . Some of the early Greek Christian theologians subjected the God of the Bible to the same 'purifying' procedure. . . . This means that Yahweh was not accepted in his proper identity; through allegoric interpretation and philosophical distillation, his disturbing concreteness was concealed behind an eternal 'essence' " (Míguez Bonino, *Christians and Marxists,* p. 39).

38. Historically, for example, dogmatic explanation of the meaning of the Christian sacraments adopted the contemporary terminology of *hylomorphism,* distinguishing a matter and a form in each of the sacraments. Just as a material principle and a formal principle were posited in the human being: a corporeal body and a spiritual soul. As philosophy, the use of this scheme for explaining the whole empirical universe is out-of-date. That does not mean that the older formulas about the sacraments are mistaken. It means that they must be poured into different molds to be directly understood today; or else that one must undertake an explanation of the older molds, making clear that they do not canonize a specific philosophy.

39. From the very beginning of this series I have stressed that it is not meant to be a work of theology. Readers interested in further clarifications along theological lines would do well to consult relevant theological manuals or studies. Here I am simply trying to provide readers with some basic elements so that they may understand the key used in the course of Western history to explain the significance of Jesus of Nazareth down to our own day. Here is the

Chalcedon formula itself, but readers must remember that some of its seemingly plain and simple terms bear traces of the many ambiguities that have
arisen in the course of centuries of debate and discussion: "Thus, following the
holy Fathers, we all unanimously teach that one must profess one only and
selfsame Son, our Lord Jesus Christ, he being complete in divinity
and . . . complete in humanity, God truly and . . . truly human being, . . .
consubstantial with the Father with respect to divinity and . . . consubstantial
with us with respect to humanity, . . . that one must recognize one only and
selfsame Christ, Son, Lord, only begotten in two natures, without confusion,
without change, without division, without separation, the difference of natures
being in no way at all erased on account of the union . . . and meeting in one
sole person and one sole hypostasis, not parted nor divided into two persons,
but one sole and selfsame only begotten Son, God, Word, Lord Jesus
Christ . . . " (DS:148).

I use the Spanish translation of Denzinger, *El magisterio de la Iglesia*. Note
that this translation leaves practically untranslated the most ambiguous term
of all: one sole *hypostasis*. It is equivalent to our terms 'substance' or 'subsis-
tence'. The term led to talk about the 'hypostatic union' of two natures in
Christ. There can be no doubt that the term is somehow trying to make clear
that Jesus Christ, the Son of God, constituted one sole being, not a transient or
mere juxtaposition of two more or less complete natures or substances. Moreover, the significance and depth of this union had already been brought out by
definitions prior to Chalcedon. They unanimously affirm the permanence of
this union forever, even after redemption had been accomplished (see DS:13,
54, 73, 86, etc.). That is the point suggested by the phrase in the Creed: 'and his
kingdom will have no end'.

40. It is true that those who accepted, or still accept, the convergence and
compatibility of Christian theology and the achievements of the Greek philosophers (Plato and/or Aristotle) should logically judge as excessive or even
'barbarous' the price paid by the Chalcedon formula to avoid the two great
alternatives that threaten it with contradiction. But we must remember that the
very same difficulty existed, even before the problem of Jesus came to the fore,
between Greek thought (however much purified or even precisely insofar as
purified) and the biblical conception of a God manifesting God's essence only
through historical acts on behalf of Israel. I have already alluded to the
difficulty of reconciling the Greek philosophical idea of God with the *fact* of
the creation of the universe (see note 32). It will be even more difficult to
reconcile the *fact* of the Incarnation with the idea of divine immutability (see
note 46).

41. Note that this dogma about language had been defined at the Council of
Ephesus, even better known for one of the special questions raised in this area:
Should Mary be regarded as the mother of Jesus, of the human nature of the
Son of God, or as the Mother of God (*theotokos*)? A simple argument
advanced to answer that question was that women are called mothers in terms
of the person of their children rather than in terms of their nature. Ephesus

opted for that linguistic argument, in line with the 'communication of languages' to which I have alluded and which was the overall theme that the Council had to resolve.

42. See the comments of Míguez Bonino cited earlier in this chapter.

43. When we read Feuerbach's *The Essence of Christianity* from this vantage point, we do not get the impression that we are reading an attack, though that is certainly what Feuerbach had in mind. That the Christian faith has led human beings to project their human ideal essence onto the divine plane *in this way* is not, *a priori* at least, an argument for the falseness of the Christian faith. For the Christian, that projection would be the result of a process of learning to learn, of deutero-learning, in which the Absolute itself is thoroughly engaged. What is questionable and unacceptable in Feuerbach's work, aside from certain aspects of this 'projection' presented by him, is his view of it as belonging to a universal, abstract human *subject*. It is the Hegelian stamp, criticized by Marx himself, that is objectionable. That stamp prevents Feuerbach from seeing that each age has different humanist 'projections', and indeed that each human being projects its own Absolute in relation to its social context. Christianity is not a sort of general convergence of all these projections; it is the one present and justified in Jesus of Nazareth, to which all christologies must return if they are to be suitable and adequate.

44. See the verse of Jorge Manrique in the Introduction, pp. 3–4, above.

45. It is paradoxical and noteworthy that the Hebrew religion always had to defend itself before Greek philosophy for the 'anthropomorphisms' of its conception of God—without noticing, perhaps, that the Greek conception of the divine, under the pretext of perfection and purity, did not even get up to the level of human likenesses but thought of God solely in terms of *things*. For example, note the impossibility, acknowledged by Thomas Aquinas, of the creator God's relating himself to his creatures: "Thus, in God there is no real relationship with creatures. On the other hand, in creatures there is a real relationship with God because creatures are subjected to the divine order and dependence on God is of their nature" (*Summa Theologica*, I, q.28, a.1 ad 3). The conclusion deduced there is that God's paternity is not a real relationship, merely a mental one.

46. It is astonishing to see how the very division of tracts in the teaching of theology permits people to bypass the most radical problems. The tract on God asserts God's absolute immutability, i.e., God's essential incompatibility with any change, internal change at the least. The tract on the Incarnation begins with the divinity of Jesus and his two natures. But the *carne* ('flesh', or here, 'human nature') in the term *Incarnation* is the predicate of the verb 'be' or, more correctly, 'come to be', whose subject is none other than God the Word: "The Word came to be flesh" (Jn 1:14). Does this imply a change in God, or has nothing changed? Significantly, the question does not come up when dealing with God in Thomas Aquinas's *Summa Theologica*, for example. Aquinas, who begins each question with objections, does not allude to 'creation', much less to the 'Incarnation', when he is dealing with God's immutability. But both

terms, especially the second, allude to a *change,* since *Incarnation* is a type of change. If one says that God did not change in becoming incarnate, then that means, to be quite blunt about it, that the Incarnation never took place.

47. I think this formulation picks up the soundest thrust and approach adopted by John A. T. Robinson with respect to this problem in *Honest to God* (see his Chapter 4). On the other hand, I think Robinson confuses the functions of iconic language and digital language when he rejects all language that would talk of a God 'outside'. It seems to me that 'outside' is a metaphor needed to avoid a more technical term like '*trans*cendence', which means the same thing. And though the notion of transcendence may be extended in crude and incorrect ways, it is the only way we have of expressing the fact that someone has us under obligation, that we are responsible to someone, that we are 'debtor-beings' in Heidegger's term.

48. Another important grammatical reason for talking about 'change' in the Incarnation is the use of the Greek aorist. This refers to snapshot action rather than a permanent situation, to something that took place at a definite point in the past.

49. It makes little difference here to note correctly that the whole of John's Gospel is more pronouncedly postpaschal in some sense than the Synoptics. The point here is that even after the paschal events, it attributes the *manifestation* of Jesus' divine 'glory' to his more human attributes, rather than to his superhuman ones, as they showed up before his resurrection. It is true that John sees the washing of the feet of the disciples and everything that surrounds the Last Supper as a sort of 'spoken' passion, a talked-out version in which Jesus tries to make clear to his disciples the meaning of the 'silent' passion that will take place soon after. But it is important to note that the washing of the feet, as a sign, does not go beyond the meaning of the passion; in itself and its signifying content, it does not include the Resurrection.

50. Especially when we include the subsequent statement contained in the hymn that Paul cites (according to the majority of exegetes): "It pleased God to have dwell in him all His fullness" (Col 1:19).

51. The usual translation, 'like God', can lead people astray insofar as the original Greek, depending on whether the word 'God' is accompanied by the definite article or not, designates the Father *(ho theos)* or the divinity *(theos).* Note the difference implied in the first verse of the Prologue of John's Gospel: " . . . the Word was with *ho theos,* and the Word was *theos"* (Jn 1:1).

52. In this example, more science fiction than not, the *fixity* of human nature would obviously mean that the experimenter would appear to be less fully human, at least so long as his ant-experience lasted. But we must remember that the term 'nature' does not designate this fixed limitation when it applies to God. Then it refers to the totality of being that is placed at the disposal of God's freedom. Any form of being, compatible with what God's freedom has chosen to be—say, 'goodness and fidelity' in the realm of values, and giving itself a specific real 'form'—is perfectly capable of being called 'divine nature' in all its fullness as such.

53. See the commentary of the *Jerusalem Bible* cited on p. 33 above, which talks about 'generosity, fidelity and power'. In reality, the Bible tends to use the first two terms as essential attributes of God, both of which point to values. The third comprises no value in itself. It is the possibility or capability, possessed by the one who possesses the total fullness of being, of *realizing* those values in the way deemed useful.

54. That is the claim of Camus, as we saw in Volume I (*Faith and Ideologies,* pp. 84–85, note 15). I again cite relevant sections of his comments here:

> That transcends, as the saying goes, the human scale; therefore it must be superhuman. But this 'therefore' is superfluous. There is no logical certainty here. There is no *experimental* probability either. All I can say is that, in fact, that transcends my scale. If I do not draw a negation from it, at least I do not want to found anything on the incomprehensible. I want to know whether I can live *with what I know and with that alone.* . . .

But if all we know experimentally are facts, then the world of values used to structure values for action will remain a closed book. And once it opens the slightest bit, we are confronted with 'transcendent data' that transcend the scale of any individual human being.

Chapter II: Christological Vacuum? Praising, Reverencing, and Serving God

55. I cite the texts of Ignatius Loyola from the one-volume *Obras completas* published by B.A.C., henceforth abbreviated as OC. I have altered the grammar and vocabulary slightly here and there for the sake of clarity. The numbers of parentheses are the now classic enumeration of the Exercises section by section. Obviously, all italics in the texts of Ignatius are mine.

Translator's Note: In this English edition I use the careful translation provided by Louis J. Puhl, S.J., *The Spiritual Exercises of St. Ignatius*; see the entry SE in the Reference Bibliography. Where it seems appropriate, a Spanish term is provided or a clarifying comment is offered. English-language readers will find many informative 'Notes on the Translation' in SE, pp. 162–98.

56. My interest is not that of the historian, and I take the Exercises as they were published. I mentioned earlier, however, that there were two main stages in their writing (Manresa and Paris), and it is worth noting that the most conspicuous christological 'absences' show up in the materials that probably date from the time of Ignatius's theological studies in Paris. The only exception is the First Week, which in all likelihood derives from his spiritual experiences in Manresa. Taken as a whole, nevertheless, the Exercises are remarkably homogeneous.

57. "The serene, lyrical intonation of the First Principle and Foundation, clear and logical as an article in Aquinas's *Summa Theologica,* seems to exude modes of scholastic speculation as found in some of its most perfect models" (P. de Leturía, in OC, p. 184).

58. It is certainly not surprising that in this concept of a test one would be

careful to itemize something that has to do with 'reverence' or fear: the difference between venial sin and mortal sin (35–37, 41). The 'reverence' will be all the greater, the more "I so subject and humble myself as to obey the law of God our Lord in all things, so that not even . . . to save my life here on earth, would I consent to violate a commandment, whether divine or human, that binds me under pain of mortal sin" (165).

59. See Gaston Fessard, *De l'actualité historique,* II, 65.

60. Some thirty years after Ignatius dies, we find Báñez, Molina, and their respective followers arguing subtly about the cruel conditions under which this decisive test takes place, a test inevitably imposed on the free human being by virtue of its condition as creature. The central point of the controversy, if not exactly predestination at this point, was something existentially very close to it: i.e., the Creator's knowledge of what would be done by a freedom situated between commands and prohibitions.

Chapter III: Christological Vacuum? Making Ourselves Indifferent

61. See Chapter I of this volume. I ask readers to remember that by 'christological vacuum' I am not alluding to the mere fact that Christ occupies more or less space in the meditations of the Exercises, much less to the fact that one or another meditation says a lot or little about him in general. By 'christological vacuum' I mean something that goes far deeper and merits more serious consideration: i.e., that theological elements, which should have been thoroughly and radically affected by christology, were not affected by it at all and remained unchanged.

62. See Karl Rahner, "The Theological Concept of Concupiscentia," *Theological Investigations I,* pp. 347–82, especially pp. 374–82.

63. For reasons of language and inner logic, I prefer to go along with that great expert on the Exercises, J. Roothaan, and read *efecto* ('effect') here rather than *afecto* ('affect'). But the force of my argument is not influenced by either reading.

Translator's Note: The comment of Louis Puhl in SE on this matter may interest readers:

'As if every attachment had been broken' *(que todo lo dexa en affecto).* Cf. Calveras and *Monumenta Historica,* p. 360. Father Roothaan thought that *en affecto* might be a copyist's error for *en effecto.* However, all manuscripts have the former and it affords an excellent meaning as the authors cited show. (SE, p. 181)

64. The case is cited by Thomas H. Clancy, S.J., "Feeling Bad about Feeling Good," *Studies in the Spirituality of Jesuits,* January 1979, 11:6.

65. Schubert M. Ogden, *The Reality of God,* pp. 17–18. "They generally contend . . . that God is the metaphysical Absolute, whose only relation to the world is wholly external . . . " (ibid., p. 18).

66. See also note 32 above. For the already indicated reason that the Church

was caught up in the process of civilizing barbarian peoples after the fall of the Roman Empire. Hence the Church felt obliged to utilize Old Testament elements, and to pass over in silence some specifically Christian elements.

67. Pierre Teilhard de Chardin, *The Divine Milieu,* p. 22: "But what will count, up there, what will always endure, is this: that you have acted in all things *conformably* to the will of God. God obviously has no need of the products of your busy activity, since He could give Himself everything without you. The only thing that interests Him . . . is the faithful use of your freedom, and the preference you accord Him over the things around you. . . . You are on a testing-ground. . . . You are on trial. So that it matters very little what becomes of the fruits of the earth. . . . If worldly aims have no value in themselves, you can love them for the opportunity they give you of proving your constancy to God."

68. One single christological example will suffice to make us ponder the conception of the law in the Exercises: "Jesus interiorized the law. He put religious intention at the center of his every action; at the center of every religious action, love; at the center of every act of love, the absolute" (Xavier Léon-Dufour, *Les Évangiles et l'histoire de Jésus,* p. 416). There are glaring similarities and dissimilarities between this statement and the corresponding conception in the Exercises.

Chapter IV: The Christology Underlying the Imitation of Christ

69. See OC, p. 283.

70. One cannot legitimately ask what importance Ignatius gave to the 'historical Jesus', since that was not a problem for his time. One can, on the other hand, recognize the importance he gave in the meditations of the Exercises to penetrating into Jesus' 'history'. But Ignatius lets into that history everything narrated in the Gospels, even in John's Gospel, whether it be *pre*paschal or *post*paschal.

71. Ignatius's stress on the details of journeys, places, and so forth, which is an obvious feature of the various 'compositions of place', does not have a historical purpose or any immediate imitational point. The details are meant to make readers feel more forcefully and subjectively the scene, 'as though present' (112, 192, 202).

72. J. Roothaan, *Adnotationes,* p. 7.

73. Hence the suggestive general title of the Exercises: "Spiritual Exercises, which have as their purpose the *conquest of self* and the regulation of one's life in such a way that no decision is made under the influence of any inordinate attachment" (21).

Chapter V: Demythologization and Discernment of Spirits

74. OC, p. 285. Ignatius permits an exception when a person cannot possibly leave his habitual occupations. He is undoubtedly thinking of public officials and men of the Church (19).

75. If everything seems to be in order, Ignatius suggests some change in the kind of penance, such as in food, sleep, or whatever: "Since God our Lord knows our nature infinitely better, when we make changes of this kind, He often *grants each one the grace to understand what is suitable for him*" (89).

76. I am not unaware of the fact that the problem commonly known as demythologization, strictly speaking, does not have to do with *mystical* language: i.e., the analogical or metaphorical descriptions of subjective divine phenomena or *inner* divine phenomena in the human soul. See my remarks at the start of this chapter. But insofar as such phenomena are regarded as a 'revelation' of criteria for some concrete action in the outside world, then the criterion adduced for that action would have to be 'mythical'. That is precisely what happens in the Exercises. The explanation of the choice made appeals to an immediate communication of God's will, which is strictly similar to the gospel explanation for the flight of Joseph, Mary, and the child Jesus into Egypt (Mt 2:13.19).

77. "This was the way preferred by St. Ignatius and used frequently by him in his own life. The most typical example is the choice he made to see whether the sacristies of the professed houses should have income or not. The feelings and even visions he had on that occasion are recorded in his famous spiritual diary. . . . *Its use calls for no little experience* in the way of the spirit and *much light* and prudence in the director" (OC, p. 233; see my Appendix in this volume).

78. This latter comment is only a supposition, based not only on the common practice of Ignatius and his companions but also on the already indicated conception that the Fourth Week should somehow correspond to the unitive way (10), and hence, at most, to a 'confirmation' of the choice made. Thus, the appropriate place for choosing a way of life would be the stage known as the illuminative way, which takes in the Second Week and the Third Week.

79. See in the autograph *directorio,* Chap. I, n. 11 (OC, p. 279); Chap. III, n. 18 (OC, p. 281). Also see 324 and 329 in the Exercises themselves.

Chapter VI: King—Kingdom—Reign

80. In my opinion, this was the mistake of the Reformation, in a controversy flubbed by both sides: i.e., to assume that God's love for human beings was better manifested in the acceptance and even passivity of the latter, as if an essential dimension of love were not attaching importance to the decisions of the person loved. The cause of this defect was undoubtedly the confusion of two things, a confusion not sufficiently forestalled by Catholic theology: i.e., the activity of the human being on the one hand and the anxiety to ensure one's salvation through the works of the law on the other. As I noted in Volume III, we find a much more balanced conception of this matter, even within Protestant theology, in the comment of Reinhold Niebuhr *(The Nature and Destiny of Man,* I, 272): "Without freedom from anxiety man is so enmeshed in the vicious circle of egocentricity, so concerned about himself, that he cannot release himself for the adventure of love." Moreover, the conception of a

historical project common to both God and the human being was as absent from the theology of the Counter Reformation as it was from that of the Reformation.

81. We must remember that the Counter Reformation proved incapable of seeing the profound, albeit incomplete, analysis of Paul made by Luther and many of his followers. It is not so surprising or strange that the christology of Paul is absent from the Exercises and its basic elements.

82. As we have seen in Volume II, exegesis tells us that the gospel word usually translated as 'kingdom' would be more correctly translated as 'reign': i.e., the actual, effective fulfillment of the king's will in the structure of the society of his charge, or, the carrying out of his kingdom's program or 'standard'.

83. I say 'paradoxically' because the Letter to the Hebrews lays the justifying basis for the cessation of all cultic sacrifice. Jesus, with his unique sacrifice, obtained once and for all from God all that we might need from God until the end of time (Heb. 10:11–14).

84. This is the interpretation accepted by Iparraguirre: "St. Ignatius uses the term in the more medieval sense offered by St. Thomas and St. Bernard: as subjection and subordination to God, without any rebelliousness against what has been determined by divine law" (OC, p. 230).

85. Here we obviously cannot take advantage of the list of contemplations dealing with Christ that are taken literally from the Gospels. Not because a christology would have nothing to say about them, but purely and simply because they are not *proper* or peculiar to the Exercises as such. I have already considered what frames them and gives them their specific orientation and import.

Chapter VII: Conclusion: The Tensions of a Christology

86. It is certainly true that there is a clear Greek influence in the Bible, particularly in some deuterocanonical books such as the Book of Wisdom; but such cases are exceptional. The statement that in the Bible God does not assume the features shown by the historical Jesus calls for further specification, which I will introduce in dealing with the third element.

87. By this I mean that the curious survival of Greek philosophy in a world where its corresponding culture had practically disappeared more than likely was due, in my opinion, to the ideological function served by that philosophy vis-à-vis the division of labor and the structuring of society.

88. The word alludes etymologically to the desert *(erēmos)*. The same is true of other words, not all contemporary, used to designate anchorites and monks *(monacus)*. They suggest solitude as a rejection of the existing society. It is true that these 'protesters' later reentered urban life, in a way, by living in monasteries. But this was a slow process that ever remained incomplete. Even ouside the desert, monasteries and convents were forms of an artificially created solitude that was protected by vows, rules, cloister, etc.

89. The original context is marked by a crucial fact: Jesus' own life is an 'active' one. But in Luke 10:38–42, we find Jesus visiting Martha and Mary in Bethany. Martha is busy making preparations for the meal. Her sister, Mary, stays at Jesus' feet and listens to him instead of worrying about meal preparations or helping Martha. When Martha complains, Jesus tells Martha that Mary has chosen the better part, and that it will not be taken from her. For centuries, prescientific exegesis saw an allegory here, elevating Jesus' comment in a concrete, personal context into an abstract and atemporal principle. This is the only text that St. Thomas could adduce to support the supposed primacy of the contemplative life over the active life.

90. See *Summa Theologica,* II–II, q.182.

91. I think it is totally pointless to dissociate the conception of God from christology, or to evaluate the conception of God separately at least, as Jon Sobrino seems at first glance to try to do. It is true that Sobrino, in examining 'The Christ of the Ignatian Exercises', admits that "the God of Jesus is a different God who can be known only through Jesus" *(Christology at the Crossroads,* p. 417). But with respect to the use of God at key points in the Exercises, such as in the First Principle and Foundation, Sobrino's argument is that our dissatisfaction with it stems from the fact that "our culture is largely profane rather than sacral" (ibid., p. 414). But why lose the criterion in this way and approve a christology that is incapable of profoundly affecting the concept of God? In my opinion, Sobrino does not point up the flaws and failings of the christology in terms of its task of revealing the being of God.

92. Here I am not using the term 'popular' *[popular]* in the current Latin American sense applied to *religiosidad 'popular'* or *cristianismo 'popular'*: i.e., referring to the religious belief or practice of the lowest classes in society. By 'popular' here I mean nonacademic Christianity as it was lived in practice and at every social level, though it may have taken distinct forms at each level.

93. The spirituality of the Exercises, despite their christological dependence on the *Imitation of Christ,* is not monastic but basically a lay spirituality such as that presented by Manrique. This becomes clear in the new form that Ignatius and his companions will give to the Society of Jesus. It will distinguish their Society very clearly from the great religious orders in existence up to then, although theirs would not be the only one of this sort in their age. Moreover, the group formed by Ignatius would hesitate and deliberate seriously before accepting the minimum framework of the religious life in legal terms: i.e., the three vows of poverty, chastity, and obedience. And the criterion in their deliberation would be the compatibility of such a life with the historical design that all had drawn from the practice of the Exercises.

94. It should not be surprising that this mistake was not denounced or corrected. As is natural and human, the Church is far less concerned about mistakes that favor it in some way.

95. See the Appendix of this volume for a discussion of the ways in which such 'undertakings' or 'enterprises' would transform the manner of making a good choice that is derived from the Exercises.

96. Thus, when he deemed it suitable, Francis Xavier would shift from a life of extreme poverty to the ostentatious trappings of his mission as papal nuncio.

Appendix: A Christology Encounters History

97. See OC, pp. 781–82.

98. Ibid., pp. 785–90, especially pp. 788–89.

99. Ibid., p. 661.

100. *Monumenta Ignaciana,* series I, Volume II, letter 1061 (dated February 14, 1550), p. 684. The OC I cite in this volume is a one-volume edition. It obviously could only provide a selection of the 7,000 letters by Ignatius or his secretaries that are included in the *Monumenta Ignaciana.* The criterion of that selection was to limit it to "those [letters] that offer some interesting aspect of Ignatius's personality" (OC, p. 610). If that was indeed the guiding criterion, rather than some other one, it would be interesting to know why the letter I cite in the text of the Appendix was not included in the OC selection.

101. OC, p. 738.

102. Ibid., p. 739, n. 3.

103. Ibid., p. 727.

104. This is clearly evident in the Constitutions (see OC, pp. 429, 430, 436, 474, 475).

105. Ignatius contemplated this seriously, as we learn from his autobiography, n. 71 (OC, p. 128).

106. This argument or hypothesis could be backed up by showing how, in fact, the practice of the Exercises, from the days of Ignatius, provided vocations to the Society of Jesus and not to other religious orders in general. We would have to isolate the fact from the 'variables' alluded to. Above all, we would have to prove that this attraction does not derive from the Exercises as such but rather from the later development that the religious order founded by Ignatius gives to that spirituality. That is my hypothesis. If it is correct, it would mean that the search for the *foundational charism* of the Society of Jesus should not center around the Exercises, which are much more general or universal than the former, but around the gradual construction of the specific project that gave rise to the Society of Jesus and put the Exercises in its service.

107. Iparraguirre's Introduction to the correspondence (OC, p. 600). He goes on to say: "If you bring together the norms and counsels of spiritual teaching that St. Ignatius gives in his letters, you will have a treatise on perfection and a *reliable interpretation* of the major principles of the Exercises" (OC, p. 602; my italics).

108. OC, pp. 784–85.

109. OC, p. 785.

110. OC, p. 650.

111. Iparraguirre's Introduction, OC, p. 304.

112. "The way that our Father [*Ignatius*] operated at the time of the Constitutions was to say Mass every day, present the point to God, and pray over it" (Gonçalves de Camara). See OC, p. 309.

113. OC, p. 653.

114. OC, p. 309.

Reference Bibliography

1. Works Cited by Abbreviations

DS. Denzinger, Bannwart, and Schoenmetzer. *Enchiridion Symbolorum*. Segundo cites the Spanish edition: *El magisterio de la Iglesia,* Barcelona: Herder, 1955.

GS. *Gaudium et spes*. Vatican II, Pastoral Constitution on the Church in the Modern World, December 7, 1965.

JB. *The Jerusalem Bible*. Eng. trans., Garden City, NY: Doubleday, 1966.

OC. Ignatius of Loyola. *Obras completas*. One-volume edition. Madrid: B.A.C., 1963.

SE. Louis J. Puhl, S.J. *The Spiritual Exercises of St. Ignatius*. A New Translation Based on Studies in the Language of the Autograph. Westminster, MD: Newman Press, 1951. Reprint available from Loyola University Press, Chicago.

2. Works Cited by Title

The Imitation of Christ. Thomas à Kempis. Numerous editions.

3. Works Cited by Author

Aquinas, T. *Summa Theologica.*

Bateson, G. *Steps to an Ecology of Mind*. New York: Ballantine Books, 1972.

Botterweck, G. J. *Gott erkennen*. Bonn: P. Hanstein Verlag, 1951.

Camus, A. *The Myth of Sisyphus and Other Essays*. Eng. trans., New York: Knopf, 1969.

Clancy, T. H. "Feeling Bad about Feeling Good," *Studies in the Spirituality of Jesuits,* January 1979, 11:6.

Dorr, Donal. *Spirituality and Justice*. Maryknoll, NY: Orbis Books, 1984.

Duquoc, C. *Cristología: Ensayo dogmático sobre Jesús de Nazaret*. I: El Mesías. Sp. trans., Salamanca: Ed. Sígueme, 1972.

Fessard, G. *De l'actualité historique*. Bruges: Desclée de Brouwer, 1960.

Feuerbach, L. *The Essence of Christianity*. Eng. trans., New York: Harper & Row, 1957.

Galilea, S. "Liberation Theology and New Tasks Facing Christians," Chapter VIII in Gibellini (see next entry).

Gibellini, R. (ed.). *Frontiers of Theology in Latin America,* Eng. trans., Maryknoll, NY: Orbis Books, 1978.

Gutiérrez, G. *A Theology of Liberation*. Eng. trans., Maryknoll, NY: Orbis Books, 1973.

143

———. *We Drink from Our Own Wells: The Spiritual Journey of a People.* Eng. trans., Maryknoll, NY: Orbis Books, 1984.

Jaeger, W. *Paideia: The Ideals of Greek Culture.* Three volumes. Eng. trans., New York: Oxford University Press, 1943–1945.

Léon-Dufour, X. *Les Évangiles et l'histoire de Jésus,* Paris, 1963. Eng. version, *The Gospels and the Jesus of History,* New York: Doubleday Image Books.

Machoveč, Milan. *A Marxist Looks at Jesus.* Eng. trans., Philadelphia: Fortress Press, 1976.

Manrique, J. *Coplas por la muerte de su padre* (c. 1476). Spanish text with plain prose translation in J. M. Cohen (ed.), *The Penguin Book of Spanish Verse,* Baltimore: Penguin Books, 1960.

Míguez Bonino, J. *Christians and Marxists.* Eng. trans., Grand Rapids, MI: Eerdmans, 1976.

Niebuhr, R. *The Nature and Destiny of Man.* Two volumes. New York: Scribner's, 1964.

Ogden, S. *The Reality of God.* New York: Harper & Row, 1977.

Pannenberg, W. *Jesus—God and Man.* Second edition. Eng. trans., Philadelphia: Westminster Press, 1977.

Rahner, K. "The Theological Concept of Concupiscentia," *Theological Investigations I.* Baltimore: Helicon Press, 1961, pp. 347–82.

Robinson, J. A. T. *Honest to God.* Philadelphia: Westminster Press, 1963.

Roothaan, J. *Adnotationes.* The Hague, 1971.

Segundo, J. L. *An Evolutionary Approach to Jesus of Nazareth.* Volume V of Jesus of Nazareth Yesterday and Today. Eng. trans., Maryknoll, NY: Orbis Books, forthcoming.

———. *Faith and Ideologies.* Volume I of Jesus of Nazareth Yesterday and Today. Eng. trans., Maryknoll, NY: Orbis Books, 1984.

———. *Grace and the Human Condition.* Volume 2 of A Theology for Artisans of a New Humanity. Eng. trans., Maryknoll, NY: Orbis Books, 1973.

———. *The Historical Jesus of the Synoptics.* Volume II of Jesus of Nazareth Yesterday and Today. Eng. trans., Maryknoll, NY: Orbis Books, 1985.

———. *The Humanist Christology of Paul.* Volume III of Jesus of Nazareth Yesterday and Today. Eng. trans., Maryknoll, NY: Orbis Books, 1986.

———. *The Liberation of Theology.* Eng. trans., Maryknoll, NY: Orbis Books, 1976.

Sobrino, J. *Christology at the Crossroads: A Latin American Approach.* Eng. trans., Maryknoll, NY: Orbis Books, 1978.

Teilhard de Chardin, P. *The Divine Milieu.* Eng. trans., New York: Harper & Row, 1960.

Von Rad, G. *Estudios sobre el Antiguo Testamento.* Spanish trans., Salamanca: Ed. Sígueme, 1975. German original, *Gesammelte Studien zum Alten Testament,* Munich, 1958.

———. *Old Testament Theology.* Two volumes. Eng. trans., New York: Harper & Row, 1962.

General Index

Compiled by James Sullivan

Other Orbis Titles. . .

FAITH AND IDEOLOGIES
Vol. 1, Jesus of Nazareth Yesterday and Today
by Juan Luis Segundo
The first of a five-volume liberation christology that considers how the church should interpret Jesus against the background of oppression and despair in Latin America. As an anthropology, not a theology, this work sets the stage for the christological discussion to follow. Here Juan Luis Segundo analyzes various aspects of human existence, such as trust in life, religion, dogma, science, Marxism, and social development in industrial and Latin American societies, in terms of faith and ideology.

"Segundo has in this book excelled all his previous work."
The National Catholic Reporter

no. 127-6   368pp. pbk.

THE HISTORICAL JESUS OF THE SYNOPTICS
Vol. 2, Jesus of Nazareth Yesterday and Today
by Juan Luis Segundo
In his monumental 5-volume series, *Jesus of Nazareth Yesterday and Today*, Juan Luis Segundo attempts to place the person and message of Jesus before us all, believer and unbeliever alike. He shakes off the christological dust of previous centuries so that we can hear the words that Jesus spoke. Having set forth his terms and methodology in Volume 1 (*Faith and Ideologies*), Segundo, in Volume 2, develops a novel approach to a classic theological pursuit—the quest for the historical Jesus.

Drawing upon his solid grasp of contemporary New Testament scholarship, Segundo explores the meaning of Jesus' parables as well as his proclamation of the kingdom of God, as they are recorded in the synoptic gospels. The result is insightful and challenging exegesis, which enables the reader to see Jesus of Nazareth "as a witness to a more humane and liberated human life," whose message of effective love is imbued with both religious and political significance. This book is essential reading for scholars and advanced students in religion.

no. 220-5   240pp. pbk.

THE HUMANIST CHRISTOLOGY OF PAUL
Vol. 3, Jesus of Nazareth Yesterday and Today
by Juan Luis Segundo
For Juan Luis Segundo, the first eight chapters of Romans "embody the most complete and complex synthesis offered by Paul about the significance of Jesus Christ for the human being." This groundbreaking exegesis focuses chiefly on Paul's treatment of sin,

faith, and the impact of their interaction on human existence. Segundo reveals new elements in Paul's christology that help us to see the central problem of our contemporary situation: "the creation and maintenance of structures and power-centers that are bound to block all effective forms of loving our neighbors in either the public or private sector."

"As a political scientist sympathetic to the theological argument of the liberationists, I have been worried by the naivete of much of their political analysis. Segundo's exploration of Romans is provocative and exciting. Paul's apparently 'apolitical' approach is shown to be extraordinarily relevant to our times. . . . A book to be read and pondered."

David Skidmore, University of York, England

no. 221-3   256pp. pbk.

FACES OF JESUS
Latin American Christologies
edited by José Míguez Bonino
The most extensive part of this book is devoted to describing and analyzing the christologies that have been present in Latin America throughout history. A fascinating picture emerges of how Jesus functions within establishment, traditional peasant, and revolutionary sectors of the population. Boff, Casalis, Segundo, Croatto, Assmann, and others contribute to this ecumenical effort.

"If one thinks, or is tempted to think, that Christian theology is boring, stale, repeating the eternal, unchanging truths, then this book will shatter the myth."   *America*

no. 129-2   192pp. pbk.

CHRISTOLOGY AT THE CROSSROADS
A Latin American Approach
by Jon Sobrino
A landmark contribution to contemporary christological thought and action that is rooted in the historical Jesus and in the Latin American situation of oppression, injustice, and exploitation.

"The most thorough study of Christ's nature based on Latin America's liberation theology."   *Time Magazine*

no. 076-8   458pp. pbk.

JESUS IN LATIN AMERICA
by Jon Sobrino
Scarcely anyone has questioned Jon Sobrino's qualifications as a theologian or the transforming efficacy of his theological work. But some have questioned its orthodoxy, as well as the orthopraxis of the activity his theological production has set afoot. Here Sobrino responds to his critics, but also obliges them to open their minds and hearts to the new wealth of christological knowledge that they seem to ignore or have forgotten. Sobrino again says that Jesus is God, but then adds at once that the only true God is the God revealed historically and scandalously in the poor.

no. 412-7   182pp. pbk.

PASSION OF CHRIST, PASSION OF THE WORLD
The Facts, Their Interpretation, and Their Meaning Yesterday and Today
by Leonardo Boff

Leonardo Boff calls *Passion of Christ, Passion of the World* a work "experimental" in nature: an attempt to explore the meaning of the cross, both as it has been interpreted in the past and how it should be interpreted in the context of contemporary faith and circumstances. The circumstances he speaks of are the poverty and repression, fear and violence under which so many of the world's people suffer today. Boff's question: In such a world, how can the cross be understood and preached—and what are the consequences of that understanding and that praxis?

"This is an important contribution from Latin America to the ongoing discussion of the theological significance of the passion of Christ in the context of the pain of the world . . . a profound and passionate reflection on the cross of Christ which takes his humanity and historical reality seriously, noting its parallels with the sufferings in which Christians are called to live their faith today. This book is therefore provocative and challenging for all who are concerned about the meaning of following Christ in the world."

Orlando E. Costas, Dean
Andover Newton Theological School

no. 563-8   160pp. pbk.
no. 564-6   160pp. cloth

JESUS CHRIST LIBERATOR
A Critical Christology for Our Time
by Leonardo Boff

"An excellent introduction to the basics of contemporary liberation Christology and thought, written from a position of deep faith . . . particularly helpful in its biblically faithful assessment of the politics of Jesus." *The Christian Century*

no. 236-1   335pp. pbk.

JESUS BEFORE CHRISTIANITY
by Albert Nolan

This portrait of Jesus is unmistakably clear, convincing, challenging, and different. We are introduced to the man as he was before he became enshrined in doctrines, dogmas, and ritual. Nothing is assumed; the historical evidence about Jesus is allowed to speak for itself. Here is a man who was deeply involved with the real problems of his time—which turn out to be the real problems of our time too.

This is the story of a Jesus who was unmistakably human. It is not until the last chapter that the author, turning many of our preconceived ideas upside down, shows us a surprisingly new way of understanding what is meant by Jesus' divinity. The book can be read profitably by anyone—the scholar, the layman, the religious, and those who no longer know whether they believe or not.

"The book is full of arresting and challenging insights for the Christian of today. Nolan's ideas are stated with passionate conviction and he has read widely and judiciously among modern exegetes of varied schools." *Catholic Herald*

no. 230-2   160pp. pbk.